Carson City Morgan Dollars

Featuring the Coins of the GSA Hoard

3rd Edition

Adam Crum • Selby Ungar • Jeff Oxman

Whitman Publishing, LLC
PUBLISHING SINCE 1934
www.whitman.com

Carson City Morgan Dollars

Featuring the Coins of the GSA Hoard

3rd edition

www.whitman.com

© 2014 Whitman Publishing, LLC
3101 Clairmont Road • Suite G • Atlanta, GA 30329

ISBN: 0794842275
Printed in the United States of America

CONTENTS

Acknowledgments iv
Foreword, by Q. David Bowers v
1. Introduction 1
2. How to Collect Carson City Morgan Silver Dollars 34
3. Carson City Morgan Silver Dollars: All Dates, Plus Selected Varieties 38
   1878-CC 39
     VAM 6 42
     VAM 11 43
     VAM 18 46
     VAM 24 49
   1879-CC 52
     VAM 3 55
   1880-CC 58
     80/79, Reverse of 78, VAM 4 61
     Reverse of 79, High 7, VAM 5 64
     Reverse of 79, Low 7, VAM 6 67
     Reverse of 78, VAM 7 70
   1881-CC 73
     VAM 2 76
   1882-CC 79
     VAM 2 82
   1883-CC 85
     VAM 4 88
   1884-CC 91
     VAM 2 94
   1885-CC 97
     VAM 4 100
   1889-CC 103
   1890-CC 106
     VAM 4 109
   1891-CC 112
     VAM 3 115
   1892-CC 118
   1893-CC 121
   1900-O/CC 124
Appendix A: Collector's Checklist 125
Appendix B: Carson City GSA Morgan Dollar Populations 127
About the Authors 129
Index 130

ACKNOWLEDGMENTS

Thank you to all of the following, who helped provide research, illustrations, and photography, and who share our passion for the coins of the Carson City Mint:

Dennis Baker   Scott Schechter
Scott Heller   Doug Sharpe
Geoff Hodes   Ben Todd
Dave Lange   Chuck Tressler
Rich Montgomery

FOREWORD
by Q. David Bowers

Morgan silver dollars—perhaps the most popular American coins ever minted! They conjure up images of cowboys in the Old West, of casino slot machines and honkytonks, of rich silver mines that seemingly overnight turned tiny Western camps into bustling young cities full of energy and promise.

Morgan dollars exist in large enough quantities that, for most dates and mintmarks, we coin collectors can contemplate and study many examples of each before buying. Some dates, however, are scarce or even rare, presenting a challenge and requiring some patience—but bringing with them the excitement of the hunt. Coin collectors love such challenges. What fun would it be if you could simply write a check and buy a prefabricated collection of Morgan dollars in one fell swoop? As I wrote in the *Guide Book of Morgan Silver Dollars*, "The thrill of the chase is what makes Morgan dollar collecting interesting and exciting, indeed all of numismatics a wonderful challenge and intellectual pursuit."

Among Morgan dollars, those of the Carson City Mint hold a special place in the hearts and imaginations of coin collectors. Many scarce and rare dates and varieties were created in this romantic Western mint.

The birth of Carson City, the excitement of the Comstock Lode, the growth of the Nevada Territory, and the development of the Carson City Mint—these stories and more are engagingly told in this new edition of *Carson City Morgan Dollars*. Authors Adam Crum, Selby Ungar, and Jeff Oxman bring to life such colorful characters as John Sutter, Sam Brannan, Mark Twain, Kit Carson, John Sherman, and Richard "Silver Dick" Bland.

Beyond that fertile history, Crum, Ungar, and Oxman explore the events and personalities involved in the discovery of hidden hoards of Carson City silver dollars, and their distribution by the federal government's General Services Administration (GSA). The 1960s were a unique time for Morgan dollar collectors. The "silver rush" began in November 1962, when a vault at the Philadelphia Mint, sealed since 1929, was opened to reveal many bags of 1903-O Morgan dollars, all Uncirculated! These were great rarities at the time—the most elusive New Orleans issue—and way back then cataloged $1,500 each in *A Guide Book of United States Coins*. However, even with this amount of money, such a coin would be hard to find. Most numismatists had never seen one.

This bonanza attracted nationwide attention, and before long other dates and mints of coins came to light, stored not only in the Philadelphia Mint, but elsewhere. Hundreds of millions of silver dollars of various dates and mints, Morgan and Peace dollar types, well worn and also Mint State, were eagerly gathered by the public. Finally, in March 1964 the vaults were empty. Empty, that is, except for about three million Carson City dollars stored in bags in the Treasury Building in Washington, DC. The government held these back and, in later sales through the GSA, made them available to collectors. Certain once-rare dates—1882-CC, 1883-CC, and 1884-CC—were now available by the hundreds of thousands, in some instances the majority of the *original mintage.* What a wonderland! Excitement prevailed. Today we can still collect and enjoy coins from the Treasury hoard, some of them packaged in special GSA holders.

The authors tell you how to collect Carson City Morgan dollars (as type coins, by date and mintmark only, and by date and variety). The silver dollars sold by the GSA are given special attention, and all of the coins are studied "by the numbers"—with original mintages, a detailed analysis of GSA holdings, rarity rankings, and condition censuses. "Collector Insights" and "Variety Notes" for each of these remarkable coins are joined by excellent photographs in actual size and close-up enlargements. The authors provide retail valuations for the silver dollars, both in their original GSA cases and in third-party slabs, in multiple Mint State grades (including Prooflike and Deep Mirror Prooflike designations).

This combination of American history, numismatic research, market reporting, census data, and collector insight makes *Carson City Morgan Dollars* a necessary volume in your silver-dollar library. Read and enjoy—and then on with the hunt!

Q. David Bowers
Wolfeboro, New Hampshire

Q. David Bowers is the award-winning author of more than 50 numismatic books, hundreds of auction and other catalogs, and several thousand articles including columns in *Coin World*, *Paper Money*, and *The Numismatist*. He is a past president of both the American Numismatic Association (1983–1985) and the Professional Numismatists Guild (1977–1979). In his 60-plus-year career in numismatics he has earned most of the highest honors bestowed by the hobby community, including the ANA's Lifetime Achievement Award and induction in the ANA Numismatic Hall of Fame. He has written extensively on the subject of silver dollars, and his *Guide Books of Morgan Silver Dollars* is a perennial best-seller.

—1—

INTRODUCTION

In 1964, the year before the discontinuation of silver coinage, an official audit of the vaults of the Treasury Building in Washington, D.C., uncovered an astounding three million U.S. silver dollars struck in the late 1800s at the historic Carson City Mint.

Though it had produced coinage for only a little over two decades, from 1870 to 1893, the U.S. Mint at Carson City, Nevada, left behind a magnificent legacy. Most coins struck at the mint are scarce to rare, some very rare. Yet no matter the rarity or market value, each coin struck at the Carson City Mint harkens back to an era in U.S. history like no other: the legendary Wild West and the great bonanza years of the late 19th century. A rich and fascinating series of events during those years culminated in the production of the Carson City Morgan dollar, a coin with an impressive historical pedigree and a unique, double-letter mintmark.

THE GREAT CALIFORNIA GOLD RUSH

John A. Sutter in 1866

A Mexican named Francisco Lopez was the first to discover gold in California, in the San Francisquito Canyon near the pueblo of Los Angeles. Yet it was another man's accidental discovery of gold, on January 24, 1848, northeast of Sacramento along the American River, that brought monumental change to what was then one of the farthest outposts of a young United States of America. Ironically, neither the discoverer, James Marshall, nor his employer, Captain John Sutter, were particularly enthusiastic about the find, since Sutter was at work establishing an agricultural empire and Marshall had a sawmill to build. As incredible as it may seem, the two men agreed to keep the gold a secret.

Predictably, however, word of the discovery eventually got out. The news was met with general disbelief at first, until one Sam Brannan, a storekeeper in Sutter's Creek, paraded a bottle filled with gold dust around San Francisco, shouting "Gold! Gold!

James Marshall in front of Sutter's sawmill in Coloma, California

Sam Brannan

Gold from the American River!" His stunt ignited the gold rush, and in just nine weeks Brannan was rewarded with a handsome profit of $36,000. But his fortune wasn't made in gold. Rather, Brannan was the first person to sell picks, pans, and shovels to the ready-made market of miners who desperately needed digging supplies.

PROMISE AND DANGER

Suddenly, California seemed to offer more promise than any other place on Earth. Gold fever had hit; businesses were forced to shut down due to a lack of employees, and the populations of many of the coastal towns were depleted as their inhabitants headed to the gold fields.

Some who traveled to California by covered wagon had absolutely no concept of the challenges that lay ahead. The tragic fate of the Donner party in 1846, for example, was a grisly lesson in the importance of correctly timing departures to avoid the Sierra Mountains in winter.

One of the two main routes to California by ship was a 17,000-mile route around South America and Cape Horn that took five to seven months, during which travelers had to deal with violent storms and sickness. The second route, via Panama by steamship, was quicker but more expensive, and in the crowded conditions of its ships sickness was a problem as well. At one point more than 500 ships were anchored in the San Francisco harbor, many abandoned by crews who had gone in search of their fortunes.

Gold Hill (top) and Silver City (bottom), mining boom-towns in Nevada

The First Arrivals

The first to arrive in the early part of 1848, along with those who were already in northern California, were often rewarded with fantastic fortunes, sometimes within a few weeks. Among the first to strike it rich was a Mexican-born Los Angeles school teacher, Antonio Coronel, who literally picked his fortune up off the ground. Three Frenchmen removed a stump from the Coloma trail and dug from beneath it $5,000 in the yellow metal. An ex-slave from Virginia named Jim Freeman and his Scottish partner, "Major" William Downie, discovered a fabulous site on the Yuba, and within four months a boom town named Downieville, with 15 hotels and 5,000 residents, sprouted up. Towns appeared everywhere almost magically overnight.

The cruel reality, however, was that by the time a half-million people rushed to California to seek their fortunes, most of the easy "placer" gold had disappeared. Sadly, most of the Forty-Niners, as they were called, found only hard work, loneliness, isolation, homesickness, struggles, temptation, bad food, physical danger, illness, and even death.

By 1852, while annual gold production had reached an all-time high of $81 million, the California Gold Rush was essentially over. Veteran prospectors, hearing of rich discoveries elsewhere, almost immediately rushed off to places like Australia, New Zealand, Colorado ("Pike's Peak or Bust"), and the Canadian Northwest. Then came news of the fabled Comstock Lode, just miles from the Carson Valley trail that many of the Forty-Niners had used a decade earlier.

THE COMSTOCK LODE

A variety of colorful stories surround the discovery of the Comstock Lode. The most intriguing involves Pat McLaughlin and Peter O'Reilly. While mining for gold in 1859, their rocker (the device used to wash soil away from the ore) constantly became clogged with a heavy, blue-gray mud. Another miner, H.T.P. "Old Pancake" Comstock, claimed they were digging on his property, but he agreed not to cause any trouble if he and his friend Emmanuel Penrod were added to the claim. Comstock named himself superintendent and soon his name became associated with the lode.

Of course, that blue-gray mud proved to be silver ore, but not before the partners had sold off their mining interests. Comstock sold his share for $10,000, invested the money in a store, lost everything, and committed suicide in Montana. McLaughlin sold his interest for $3,500, wasted the money, and worked at odd jobs for the rest of his life. O'Reilly collected dividends for a few years from his share, then sold it for $50,000, built a hotel in Virginia City, and became a dealer in mining stock. Eventually he returned to mining, lost everything, went insane, and died in a California asylum.

Three Main Periods

Regardless of how it all began, the Comstock Lode ultimately became the richest silver deposit in the United States and the most important mining discovery in America. Its fascinating and complex history can be divided into three main periods.

The "litigation years," from 1859 to 1865, involved ongoing legal actions between miners and mine owners over the boundaries of mining claims, and over whether the

The Nevada Territory Catches the Attention of President Lincoln

The wealth of the Nevada Territory and its potential to become a free state did not escape the notice of President Abraham Lincoln. While the law required the Nevada constitution to be delivered to Washington, D.C., by an official of the Nevada Territory, Lincoln was so anxious for the Nevada Territory to become a state that Nevada officials telegraphed the entire constitution to Chicago. It took Frank Bell more than 12 hours to tap it out at a cost of over $4,000. The longest telegraph communication in history was then written in long-hand and delivered to Washington.

Although the Nevada Territory had not achieved the requisite minimum population required for statehood, Congress admitted it to the Union for its vast wealth and to ensure the loyalty of its residents to the United States. Just weeks after the fall of Atlanta, Nevada joined the Union as the 36th state on October 31, 1864. Nevada contributed $45 million to the Union during the war and, together with gold from California, helped finance the defeat of the Confederacy.

The boom town of Virginia City, Nevada Territory

lode was one continuous vein of ore or many veins. During this six-year period, miners removed an estimated $50 million in ore from the earth and spent about $10 million in legal fees.

From 1865 to 1875, the San Francisco–based Bank of California dominated the "banking-crowd years." Gambling on the future of the Comstock, the bank loaned money at 2% per month, undercutting smaller, less-well-capitalized banks. Through loan defaults, the bank eventually acquired so many different types of businesses and property (along with the loathing of the populace) that it held the controlling interest in Virginia City. In addition, the banking crowd drastically reduced transportation costs when it established the Virginia and Truckee Railroad.

Comstock miners

The discovery of the richest veins of ore in 1873 led to the "Bonanza Group years." From 1875 to 1881, mining superintendents John Mackay and James Fair (among others) duplicated the tactics of the Bank of California, but unlike the bank, remained popular with the people.

The Comstock Social Order

Most of the population of the Comstock consisted of young adult, single, white males. In 1870, for example, males outnumbered females in Nevada, 32,379 to 10,112. There were few very young and elderly people.

Among residents who were foreign born, there were two large and very different groups: the Europeans and the Chinese. Considering the high levels of discrimination in the East, the acceptance of European immigrants in Nevada was remarkable. Many of the most important Comstock leaders and politicians were European by birth. Adolph Sutro had been born in Prussia, and three of the four leaders of the Bonanza Group had been born in Ireland. Chinese immigrants, however, were subjected to discrimination, the most obvious example of which being that they were forbidden to work in the mines.

Although the largest religious group by far, due to Irish immigration, was Catholic, the Comstock region was essentially secular. Up until March 1861, the region that would become the Nevada Territory was actually part of the Utah Territory, which had been heavily settled by Mormons. Tension ran high between Mormons and "Gentile" (non-Mormon) Christians; the non-Mormons, who were supposed to be living under Mormon law, preferred to live under the mining towns' secular "rules and regulations," by which difficulties were settled in a fair fight. Similar to the California Gold Rush days, men carried pistols and knives, and each man became a law unto himself.

In fact, the Mormon laws were considered so unacceptable to non-Mormons that they moved to separate and establish a new territory in the western portion of Utah. Delegates were even sent to Congress in Washington to plead their case, but with no success. Taking the matter into their own hands, the separatists drafted and adopted "A Declaration" and "Constitution" and elected a governor and a legislature. The newly elected legislature met on December 15, 1859, at Genoa, received the "first annual message" from Governor Isaac Roop, passed a number of resolutions, appointed a few committees, and never met again. Ultimately, the pursuit of wealth took priority over everything else.

The Forefront of Technological Innovation

By 1880, some of the Comstock mines, having been blasted through solid rock, reached beneath the surface for thousands of feet—the deepest of that era. Because the issues were very different from those of the California Gold Rush, mining the Comstock Lode required organized work crews, costly equipment, mining companies, and investors. It birthed one technological advance after another. The Comstock was

A mid-1870s lithograph of the deep Comstock mines, including
the square-set timbers positioned to prevent cave-ins

also dangerous, and hundreds were killed, maimed, or seriously injured beneath the surface.

In 1860, the mine owners hired mining expert Phillip Deidesheimer, a graduate of the world-famous Freiberg School of Mines, to design a safer mine. He quickly developed a deep-mining support design known as "square-set" timbering, which was based on the design of bees' honeycombs. Another innovation, which made it possible to mine more of the Comstock and caught on across the

Sutro Tunnel entrance and mule train

Virginia & Truckee Railroad

The grand International Hotel in Virginia City, circa 1890

In 1869, when the demands of the Comstock surpassed the hauling capacity of mule-drawn wagons, the Virginia and Truckee Railroad was built between Virginia City and Reno along the Truckee River. The project required nine months of work by 1,200 mostly Chinese laborers. The route ran through six tunnels whose timber supports were lined with zinc to protect them from the sparks that spewed from the trains' smokestacks. The V&T hauled 500 to 800 tons of ore down the mountain every day, returning with supplies and timber. Connected to the nation's first transcontinental railway, which was also completed that year, the Virginia and Truckee Railroad was soon transporting fancy furniture, stone for an opera house, and carved woodwork for the six-story International Hotel, along with industrial supplies and ore.

As many as 45 trains a day arrived in and departed from Virginia City. For nearly 20 years the V&T was a major political and economic factor in the growth and development of western Nevada and eastern California. During the late 1870s, V&T stockholders divided dividends in excess of $100,000 a month.

West and worldwide, was invented by J.W. Haines. A narrow-gauge railway was required to transport timber from the Lake Tahoe area to the top of Spooner summit; Haines invented the V-flume in order to float timber down to the valley floor. Once it was on the valley floor, the timber was transferred to the Virginia and Truckee Railroad—another of the Comstock's engineering wonders—and transported to supply Deidesheimer's square-set timbering.

Conditions for the miners were the impetus for further innovations. Every 100 feet down into the mines, the temperature increased five degrees Fahrenheit; at 3,000 feet below the surface, clouds of steam made it difficult to see, work time was reduced to 15 minutes per hour, and the ice allotment increased to 95 pounds a day per man. Ventilation shafts provided miners with some relief, but it wasn't enough. In the late 1860s two huge air pumps were installed to force air through pipes to cool the shafts.

In order to get water to the Comstock, an enormous pipeline was laid from the Sierra Nevada Mountains to the valleys and then up over the Virginia Range. Nearly four miles

Hoisting works at the Ophir mining operation, circa 1890

The Most Famous Unsuccessful Prospector

Author and humorist Mark Twain discovered that he wasn't particularly good at prospecting and wound up working for Virginia City's largest newspaper.

"Feet that went begging yesterday were worth a brick house today," Twain observed, as shares in mines skyrocketed from $1.50 to more than $1,500 in a little over a year. "The flush times were in magnificent flower! The 'city' of Virginia claimed a [large] population, and all day long half of this little army swarmed the streets like bees, and the other half swarmed among the drifts and tunnels of the Comstock, hundreds of feet down in the earth directly under those same streets. Often we felt our chairs jar, and heard the faint boom of a blast down in the bowels of the earth under the office."

Novelist Mark Twain

in length, the Sutro Tunnel, another critical technological achievement, drained excess water from the underground mines to the Carson River valley.

Great Fortunes to Only a Few

The Comstock's richest mine, the Ophir, lay along a claim nearly a quarter of a mile in length and was quoted at $4,000 per foot. The official value of the ore the Comstock produced from 1859 until 1882 was $305,779,612.48. However, only six out of 103 companies ever paid more dividends than they required in assessments from investors, and 97 never paid a dividend at all. The mines made only a few dozen of the thousands of individuals who rushed to the Washoe in 1859 truly wealthy.

Arriving too late for the California gold rush, Irish-born John W. Mackay walked 250 miles from San Francisco to Virginia City to try his hand at the Comstock. After working with a pick and shovel for three years, Mackay heard of a claim, one of the partners to which was fighting with Confederate troops. As the story goes, Mackay located the partner on a battlefield ablaze with gunfire and bought the man's share of the claim for $500. McKay became one of the Comstock's richest mine owners and a member of the Bonanza Group. From 1873 to 1882, two of the Bonanza Group's mines produced $105,168,859 in ore, with each of the four owners receiving $74,250,000 in dividends.

Unlike the California Gold Rush, the Comstock profits mostly benefited Western-ers. The foundries and machine shops of San Francisco and other West Coast towns worked day and night to fill orders for engines, boilers, pumps, and all kinds of machinery to be shipped to the mines. Ranchers and fruit growers in California shipped fresh produce and livestock to the boom towns. Many of the fine houses on Nob Hill in San Francisco were financed by the mining millionaires, as were the Palace and Fairmont hotels, the banks, and the office buildings. Others who made their fortunes from the Comstock Lode were named Ralston and Crocker (founders of the Bank of California), Stanford, Flood, and Fair. The Comstock Lode was also instrumental in the establishment of a magnificent American numismatic legacy.

THE U.S. MINT AT CARSON CITY, NEVADA

Abraham Curry, B.F. Green, J.J. Musser, Frank M. Proctor, and their families got a bargain when they purchased land in Carson County, a part of the Utah Territory, from mountaineer John Mankin for a paltry $500 and a few horses. Mankin had acquired the land years before from a group of Mormons when they and their leader, Brigham Young, were confronted by federal authorities over the practice of polygamy and returned to Salt Lake City.

Kit Carson, for whom
Carson City was named

Unlike his partners, who gave up their rights to the land fairly quickly, Abraham Curry had something big in mind. An industrious man of great vision, Curry wanted to establish a town—and so he did. Named after the legendary frontiersman Kit Carson, Carson City was founded about the same time as the discovery of the Comstock Lode.

A Mint Near the Comstock Lode

From the beginning, most of the ore from the Comstock was transported to the mint in San Francisco. Because the practice was expensive, risky, and of little benefit to Nevada (where simple financial transactions were a challenge due to a shortage of coins), the owners of the Comstock mines began to lobby Congress for a branch mint in the Nevada Territory.

The Treasury Department began investigating the possibility and the House Ways and Means Committee backed the idea, since a large portion of the ingots and coins produced at the San Francisco Mint was shipped abroad and lost to the U.S. economy. Although Mint director James Pollock voiced strong opposition, both the House and the Senate passed the Nevada Mint Bill on March 3, 1863.

Treasury secretary Salmon P. Chase asked Colorado congressman H.P. Bennett to investigate locations for the new mint, and the enterprising Abe Curry was quick to promote Carson City as the perfect site. The congressman selected Carson City and made Abe Curry, by now one of the most influential men in the entire region, general contractor of the new facility. A lot was purchased from James L. Riddle and Moses and Mary Job in February 1865, and on December 27 of that year the secretary of the Treasury appointed a commission to oversee the building of the mint. Then, many delays—not least of which was the ongoing Civil War—placed many obstacles and challenges in the way of the construction of the mint building. The initial delay was followed by a movement to replace the proposed mint with a federal assay office. Since this meant that coins would not actually be created at the new mint, Nevada senators James Nye and William Stewart immediately stepped in and got the original legislation renewed along with an authorization of $150,000 for the mint's construction.

Alfred Mullett Designs the Mint

Supervising architect of the Treasury Alfred B. Mullett was selected as the chief designer of the new mint. It would be the first project in his eight-year career with the Treasury Department. Mullet became one of the foremost architects of his time, and a later Treasury project—the second San Francisco Mint, known as the "Granite Lady"—became one of his greatest achievements.

Mullett designed the two-and-a-half-story building over a basement foundation. The 60-by-90-foot sandstone edifice was fashioned after both the Greek and Classical styles, which was the height of fashion in the post–Civil War era. The front elevation included a 12-by-15-foot entrance porch, and the roof of the main building was to be crowned with a brick, Italian villa–style cupola. The single-story west wing, measuring 86 by 27 feet, was designed for boiler-house operations, along with an engine room, a carpentry shop, and storage.

Alfred B. Mullett

The building materials were to come from Nevada. The Nevada State Prison would quarry the sandstone blocks for the exterior of the new mint; the brick-making would be done at the Adams Brick Works in Genoa (operated by the grandsons of John Quincy Adams); and the interior wainscoting would be milled from sugar pine from the Tahoe area.

It wasn't until July 17, 1866, three years after the House and Senate passed the Nevada Mint Bill, that the architectural drawings, specifications, and authorizing documents for the new mint arrived in Carson City. As the project had survived a delay caused by the Civil War, lingering opposition within the Treasury Department, and a movement to replace the proposed mint with a federal assay office, no time was wasted. The groundbreaking ceremony took place the following morning, July 18, and the cornerstone was laid on September 24.

Lack of Funds Continues to Plague the Project

It quickly became evident that Congress had not considered the economic realitites involved in building a new mint in the West when it authorized only $150,000—an amount that would have been sufficient to construct a similar building in the East. When Curry hired Chinese laborers in order to save money, the local citizenry was soon up in arms. He begrudgingly replaced the Chinese with only white laborers, at significantly higher wages.

On December 5, 1867, while work continued on the structure, Curry traveled to Washington and Philadelphia. He spent most of 1868 seeking additional backing for the mint. On September 11, 1868, Curry returned to Carson City with the necessary guarantees. But there were still additional challenges ahead. A bill was introduced in Congress to prohibit branch mints from refining and assaying metals; though the legislation ultimately died, it was troublesome for a time. Then finances became an issue once again, when it became obvious that the salaries authorized by the Treasury Department were too low to attract a skilled assayer, melter, and refiner for the new mint. Once again, Washington had no sense of the inflated Western economy, and eventual construction costs totaled $426,788, far exceeding the $150,000 allocated for the project.

Additional Delays Prevent the Striking of Coins

Much of the minting machinery did not arrive until November 23, 1868, because it was transported from the East by ship and had to travel around South America. While

The Carson City Mint, view of the south side (left) and east facade, circa 1879

Newly Built Mint Survives an Earthquake

As if the establishment and construction of the Carson City Mint hadn't been challenging enough, at 6:00 P.M. on December 28, 1869, the entire Carson City area was rocked by a tremendous earthquake, the biggest one anyone present could remember. Though there were a number of damaged buildings in town, the Mint was not among them. Just two weeks earlier, supervising architect A.B. Mullett had reported that in spite of problems with funding, the Mint had been built strictly according to the specifications. Since it had survived the earthquake without any signs of damage, evidently it was well built.

it appeared that the Carson City Mint would begin striking coins in 1869, there was yet another delay: the chimney couldn't be completed, due to a lack of bricks in Nevada. When the bricks did arrive, the harsh Nevada winter had begun and, as was the case each year, work on the structure came to a halt.

Finally, on December 13, the Carson City Mint was deemed complete and ready to begin production. However, there was still one more delay. No dies had arrived from Philadelphia, and Curry, now superintendent of the Mint, realized that the dies that were about to arrive were dated 1869 and would be of no value in a matter of days. Dies dated 1870 arrived by Wells Fargo Express on January 10, 1870.

First CC Coins Struck

The first coins struck at the Carson City Mint were silver dollars of the Liberty Seated type, which had been designed by Christian Gobrecht in 1836. The reverse of each piece displayed a heraldic eagle with a shield upon its breast, and beneath the eagle was Carson City's CC mintmark (chosen so there would be no confusion with the C mintmark of the then-defunct Charlotte Mint). On February 11, 1870, Mr. A. Wright, who had deposited silver at the Mint at an earlier date, received 2,303 of these dollars.

Three days later, gold eagles ($10 gold coins) were struck, followed by half eagles ($5 gold coins), both of which were also of Christian Gobrecht's design. That same day a number of double eagles ($20 gold coins), designed by James B. Longacre, were struck as well. Silver coinage continued with the half dollar on April 9 and the quarter dollar on April 20. No dimes were struck at Carson City until 1871; and because Westerners thought the denomination too small, no half dimes would ever be minted in Nevada. Several other denominations were never minted at Carson City as well, including gold dollars, quarter eagles, three-dollar gold pieces, and any coins composed of copper and nickel. The Mint coined the short-lived 20-cent piece for only two years, 1875 and 1876.

During its first few years of operation, the Carson City Mint failed to produce significant numbers of any denomination. The exception was the trade dollar, authorized in 1873 and intended almost entirely for export. This was ironic, since the Carson City Mint had been legislated into existence on the premise that, unlike coinage of the San Francisco Mint, more of its refined metal would remain in the United States. The mint also failed to produce significant numbers of coins because many of those who did choose the Nevada facility opted to receive payment in ingots rather than coins; still others found that it was more economical to have their bullion refined at the San Francisco Mint.

A frequent victim of negative newspaper reporting and politics, the Carson City Mint was subject to budget cuts and threats of closure. Those sympathetic to the mint contended that the cost of operating a mint in Nevada had been continually underestimated, while others cited the high cost of minting coins in Nevada as a reason the mint should be closed and a new mint built closer to some other center of population. It also seemed that every congressman wanted a mint in his own district.

It wasn't until 1875 that coins bearing the CC mintmark were struck in large numbers. All the U.S. mints had been charged with minting coins to replace the now-obsolete fractional paper currency; in addition, the millions of silver dollars mandated by the Bland-Allison Act of 1878 brought record activity to the Carson City Mint during the 1880s.

POLITICS AND THE MORGAN DOLLAR

It wasn't commerce and it certainly wasn't public demand that birthed the Morgan silver dollar. It was political pressure from the Western silver-mine owners that brought it into existence. There was no real need for a new silver dollar in the late 1870s. The Liberty Seated dollar, which had been nicknamed the "cartwheel" because the light reflected from its surface appeared to spin much like a wagon wheel as the coin was titled back and forth, had been legislated out of existence in 1873. It was missed by few people except the silver-mining interests, who now lobbied Congress for its return.

Ohio senator John Sherman returned from the Paris International Monetary Conference in 1867 with the belief that the United States needed to adopt a gold standard based on the metric system used by the Europeans. In 1870, Sherman introduced a bill that included the recommendations of Treasury secretary George S. Boutwell to overhaul the existing coinage statutes and move control of the U.S. mints to Washington. After being promoted through two sessions of the Senate, the bill remained under consideration in the House of Representatives for more than a year and was finally passed on February 12, 1873.

The Mint Act of February 12, 1873, demonetized silver; created and limited the trade dollar as legal tender; eliminated the standard silver dollar, half dime, three-cent piece, and two-cent piece; provided for a slight increase in the weight of the quarter, dime, and half dollar to conform to the "metric" system; and attempted to tie the United States' monetary system to the gold standard. It also ended "free coinage"—the right of anyone to have foreign silver or bullion minted into U.S. silver coins without charge. United States bonds could be redeemed only in gold, since silver was no longer a monetary metal, which made it much more difficult to pay off the U.S. national debt while benefiting the Europeans, especially the English, who were large importers of American cotton and wheat.

The bottom line for the silver-mine owners was that the act had substantially reduced the amount of silver the U.S. mints needed for coinage. Adding insult to injury, demand for silver among domestic industries was down and the German Empire under Bismarck had just adopted a gold standard (as many countries throughout the world were doing), which placed more than 8,000 tons of silver on the international market in one fell swoop.

Not Enough for the Silver-Mine Lobby

Threatened nationally and internationally, the country's silver-mine owners once again went to work lobbying Capitol Hill. The mine owners wanted legislators to regard any threat to silver as a threat to the country. It was inconsequential that hardly any of the unpopular silver dollars had circulated for years, that trade dollars were heavier and being used by the millions by importers trading in Chinese port cities, and that the Mint Bureau could buy foreign silver more cheaply. Then the country's financial institutions

Superintendent Abraham Curry Resigns

Abraham (or Abram) Van Santvoord Curry was born in 1815 in Ithaca, New York. Other than the fact that he did business in Cleveland, Ohio, not much is known about him until he arrived in the western Utah Territory in 1858. He and three partners wanted to start a mercantile business in the town of Genoa, but they found a more affordable and much larger piece of land in Eagle Valley, 15 miles to the north. Curry, who envisioned a place named Carson City, had the land surveyed and a town platted with lots divided equally among the four partners. Two of his partners gave Curry their shares of the land when they lost confidence in the future of the endeavor. The third partner sold Curry his interest for 22 pounds of butter and a pony.

Superintendent Abraham Curry

In the first of many projects, Curry dug a sandstone quarry and built the two-story Warm Springs Hotel with the sandstone. He also built the Great Basin Hotel on one of his town lots, and with the kind of enthusiasm that seemed to run rampant in the West at that time, set aside 10 acres in the middle of town for the anticipated future state-capitol building. In 1861, Curry donated the use of the second floor of his Warm Springs Hotel to the first territorial legislature. That first session of the legislature divided Nevada into counties, and Carson City became the seat of Ormsby County as well as the capitol of the new territory. The following year, the Ormsby County Commission purchased Curry's Great Basin Hotel and turned it into the county courthouse.

joined the mine owners when the United States sank into an economic depression following the Panic of 1873. Both now wanted the minting of large quantities of silver coinage for release into circulation.

Under the Specie Redemption Act, passed by Congress in 1875 and signed by President Ulysses Grant, paper currency of $1 or more would be backed by gold, and the number of "greenbacks" in circulation would gradually be reduced. In addition, any paper notes denominated at less than a dollar would be removed from circulation and replaced by silver coinage. Although this act increased the amount of silver coinage in circulation, it was not enough for the silver-mine lobby. With all the cheap silver available on the worldwide market, there was no guarantee that the U.S. Mint would purchase silver from the nation's mine owners, who believed they were owed special consideration for their financial help during the Civil War. By now, the Comstock Lode was yielding $36 million in ore annually.

Authorization for a New Silver Dollar

After several unsuccessful attempts, and while the mine owners and financial interests still weren't entirely happy and complained the bill didn't go far enough, Representative Richard Bland (D-Missouri), along with William Allison (R-Iowa), finally succeeded in getting the Bland-Allison Act passed. It was sent to President Rutherford B. Hayes's desk for signing; he promptly vetoed the bill on February 8, 1878. Congress overrode the presidential veto, and the Bland-Allison Act became law.

On January 1, 1862, Governor James W. Nye appointed Curry warden of the territorial prison. Ever the entrepreneur, Curry leased his Warm Springs Hotel as the prison site. The prisoners quarried much of the building material from the adjacent land for early Carson City buildings and later the Carson City Mint. In 1864, Curry sold the prison and the quarry to the territory for $80,000. In the same year, Curry and a partner obtained rights to build and operate a macadamized toll road between Carson and Empire City, a mill town on the Carson River. In one of his less profitable moves, Curry sold his interest in the Gould and Curry Mine on the Comstock for a few thousand dollars to men who later became wealthy from the gold and silver ore.

After eight challenging years as superintendent of the Carson City Mint, Abraham Curry resigned in September 1873 and was replaced by H.F. Rice. While Curry pursued an unsuccessful run for the lieutenant governorship of Nevada, he successfully built a complex of railroad shops for the Virginia and Truckee Railroad. A grand ball was held on July 4, 1873, in the V&T engine house to celebrate the completion of the project. On October 19, just three months later, 58-year-old Curry died of a stroke. The Carson City Mint closed for the day out of respect for its first superintendent. Despite his extraordinary accomplishments, Curry's wife Mary claimed Abe had only one dollar in his pocket when he died.

Senator John Sherman
of Ohio, circa 1870s

The act required the Treasury to purchase, at current market rates (not at a prede-termined ratio tied to the value of gold), between two million and four million dollars' worth of silver bullion every month to be coined into dollars. Since the purchasing power of a dollar in the 1880s was enormous, this action by Congress was suspicious at best. Even large purchases were generally under a dollar. In addition, some people were still bartering for goods, which didn't involve money at all. Obviously, the sup-ply of silver dollars far exceeded demand. Just the same, the bill was a successful com-promise for silver miners, and Bland became known as both "the Great Commoner" and "Silver Dick," nicknames that reflected his 25-year campaign for a bimetallic stan-dard to help both the common man and the silver miners.

"Silver Dick" Bland, the "Great Commoner"

Rep. Richard P. Bland of Missouri, circa 1870s

Richard Parks Bland was born in 1835 near Hartford, Ohio. He graduated from the Hartford Academy, then taught school for two years in Ohio. After moving to Missouri and then to California, he settled in the western portion of the Utah Territory (present-day western Nevada), where he taught school and tried his hand at prospecting and mining. Bland studied law while teaching school and, after passing the bar, set up a law practice in Virginia City and Carson City. His first elected position was as treasurer of Carson County from 1860 to 1864.

In 1865, he returned to Rolla, Missouri, where he practiced law with his brother C.C. Bland. Four years later he moved to nearby Lebanon when the railroad (a predecessor of the St. Louis and San Francisco Railroad) laid track through that town. In 1872, Bland was elected as a Democrat to the U.S. House of Representatives in the 43rd Congress. He was reelected to the House 10 times, narrowly defeated in 1894, regained his seat in 1896, and elected again in 1898. He chaired the Committee on Mines and Mining in the 44th Congress and the Committee on Coinage, Weights, and Measures in the 48th, 49th, 50th, 52nd, and 53rd Congresses.

Due to the economic depression in 1894 and the unpopularity of President Grover Cleveland's policies, many Democratic Party members concluded that free silver was the party's only hope. In the spring of 1896, "silverites" won control of numerous state delegations to the National Democratic Convention. Congressman Bland was a leading candidate for the presidential nomination, but he was hindered by prejudice against his wife's Catholicism and opposition from Populists (who the Democrats had hoped would support a free-silver nominee). Bland lost a hard-fought 1896 Democratic presidential nomination to the "great orator," William Jennings Bryan.

Bland was married to Virginia Mitchell of Rolla in 1873. The couple had six children: Theodric, Ewing, Frances, John, George, and Virginia. Bland died in 1899 while still serving his country and was buried at the Calvary Catholic Cemetery in Lebanon, Missouri.

Mint Director Anticipates the Outcome

Even before legislation was passed, U.S. Mint director Henry P. Linderman felt it wouldn't be long until the silver dollar would be issued once again. And while the story has several variations, it appears that chief engraver William Barber; one of his assistants, British engraver George T. Morgan; and outside artist Anthony Paquet began creating several different designs following Linderman's instructions that a "head of Liberty" replace the full-sized figure then in use.

After reviewing the designs of both Barber and Morgan, Linderman selected the Morgan design on February 21, 1878, because it had the lowest relief and required less power to strike. Several years later Charles Barber, son of William Barber, would basically copy the design for what would become known as the Barber dime, Barber quarter, and Barber half.

In record time, just a week after the passing of the Bland-Allison Act and after a number of design changes, the Philadelphia Mint struck the first Morgan dollars on March 7, 1878. At the first-strike ceremony, the first 10 coins struck were earmarked for various dignitaries, starting with President Rutherford Hayes. A problem developed with the initial presentation piece and it was sent to the melting room; the ceremonies continued, however, and 11 more coins were struck, the last of which was also rejected. The Hayes coin is on exhibit at the Rutherford Hayes Museum in Ohio.

These first coins were struck on polished planchets, removed by hand, and put in numbered envelopes with the intent to deliver the first coin to the president, the second to Secretary of the Treasury John Sherman, and the third to Director Linderman. After that, the press began churning out dollar coins at the rate of 80 per minute.

U.S. Mint director Henry P. Linderman   Mint engraver George T. Morgan

"The Silver Dollar Girl"

Morgan needed a model for his Miss Liberty and he persuaded a reluctant 18-year old Philadelphia schoolteacher, Miss Anna Willess Williams, to sit for him five times under the watchful eye of his friend, the famous painter Thomas Eakins. Williams's reluctance was understandable and secrecy paramount, since upstanding ladies of the time kept to childbearing and teaching.

Morgan told anyone who asked that the head of Liberty on the dollar was inspired by a classic Greek figure. Miss Williams was anonymously described by Morgan as having blond hair and blue eyes and a wonderful Grecian profile.

The press started a search for the "Silver Dollar Girl" and in 1879, a Philadelphia reporter revealed Miss Williams's secret. The identification of Miss Williams as the girl on the silver dollar brought her unwanted fame as well as offers of theatrical engagements and a great deal of mail. She rejected it all in favor of a teaching position at the House of Refuge. In 1891, she took a job teaching kindergarten philosophy at the Girls' Normal School.

The announcement that the "Goddess of Liberty" was engaged to be married brought her into the public eye once more. Possibly all the publicity was too much, and her marriage never took place. She continued her career in education and became the supervisor of Philadelphia's kindergarten schools. She retired in December of 1925 after a debilitating fall and died on April 17, 1926. The American Numismatic Association journal, *The Numismatist,* reported her passing in its May 1926 issue: "An obituary told of a Philadelphia lady whose portrait had been reproduced hundreds of millions of times: 'Miss Anna W. Williams, of Philadelphia, a retired public school teacher, whose profile was used in preparing the design of the standard silver dollar in 1878, died in her native city on April 17. Death was due to apoplexy, induced by a fall she sustained last December and she had been confined to her bed since.'"

Anna Willess Williams, as drawn from the Morgan-dollar obverse design

Anna Williams, portrait drawn from life

Within a few days, several other presses came on-line and dies were delivered to San Francisco, New Orleans, and Carson City. Silver dollars were struck from 1878 to 1921 with a precious-metal content of .77344 ounces of pure "bonanza silver" from the Comstock Lode.

A First: Designer's Initial on Both Sides

Soon after production began, the Mint was advised that the eagle should have seven tail feathers, instead of the eight with which it had been designed, and Linderman ordered the change. As a result, some 1878 Morgan dollars have eight feathers, some seven—and some show seven over eight. The seven-over-eight variety is the scarcest.

The obverse side featured a left-facing portrait of Miss Liberty. With wheat and cotton in her hair, symbolizing the reconciliation of North and South, Miss Liberty wears the liberty cap of antiquity, representing hard-won freedom. On the reverse side of the coin, surrounded by laurel to honor the nation's attainments, is a magnificent American bald eagle holding the arrows of war and an olive branch of peace in its talons.

A first, the designer's initial M appears on both sides: on the truncation of Liberty's neck on the obverse, and on the ribbon's left loop on the reverse. Mintmarks (O, S, D, and CC) are found below the wreath on the reverse.

The public's reception of the Morgan dollar was less than enthusiastic, and it was given nicknames just like those of its predecessor. Since the eagle was viewed by many as somewhat scrawny, the coins became known as "buzzard dollars," as well as "Bland dollars" and "cartwheel dollars."

The Panic of 1893

Treasury vaults overflowed with silver dollars by 1893. Yet minting steadily continued until the spring of that year, when the production of the Nevada mines began to decrease and silver prices continued to fall worldwide—this despite the fact that the powerful silver lobby continued to pressure the federal government to subsidize the U.S. silver market.

In an unbelievable turn of events, the Bland-Allison Act was modified by the Sherman Silver Purchase Act of 1890, which required the Treasury to buy 187.5 tons of domestic silver every month, this to be used only for coining silver dollars. The new act also required that mine owners be paid in Treasury notes redeemable in gold, which led to a run on the Treasury's gold supply. With the threat of a Treasury default, Wall Street panicked, and 419 banks failed. Suddenly millions of Americans were jobless and hungry. President Grover Cleveland, in a second term following Benjamin Harrison, called Congress into special session and the Sherman Act was repealed on November 2, 1893, but only after months of bitter opposition led by the infamous "Silver Dick" Bland. A total of $108,800,188 in silver bullion intended for the minting of dollars was exhausted by 1904, ending the Morgan-dollar era for 17 years. Most of these dollars, like the ones before, were either melted or remained in Treasury vaults until the 1960s.

Panic in the New York Stock Exchange on the morning of May 5, 1893

Scandals Mark the End of the Carson City Mint

Due to a combination of the slowing of silver-mine production, consistently low silver prices, and the allegation that a Carson City Mint employee had attempted to smuggle gold bullion out of the mint in a lunch box, Mint director Robert Preston suspended coining operations at Carson City on June 1, 1893.

Several high-profile trials involving the Mint were reported across the country. When it was discovered that a key witness in one of the cases had caused a hung jury because he had been bribed to keep silent, another trial was held. Ultimately, James Heney, John T. Jones, and Henry Piper, all former Mint employees, were found guilty and sentenced to lengthy prison terms.

Approximately $1.5 Million Stolen From the Mint

One day in 1894, chief melter Hirsch Harris discovered that copper had been used to replace the naturally occurring gold in a few of the Mint's silver bars. The U.S. Treasury Department initiated a full investigation when it was discovered that the gold content was missing from more bars. Any possibility of the Mint's resuming coining was destroyed in 1895, however, when several Mint employees, along with some prominent community figures, were proven to have been systematically removing gold bullion during the refining process as far back as 1892. An estimated $75,000 in gold had been stolen (approximately $1.5 million in today's dollars).

Throughout the trial, the public suspected a connection between the gold theft and the Bullion and Exchange Bank that had taken over the refining operations and even set up an office inside the Mint. When B&E president Jacob Klein defended the accused men, suspicions were reinforced. No evidence of unlawful activity on the part of B&E or its president was found. This exoneration, however, wasn't sufficient to save Klein's job.

The incident had a major impact on the country, as well as on the Mint. The scandal motivated the federal government to take major steps toward achieving more orderly, lawful operations by defining its role in oversight responsibility, business accountability, and compliance with the law. Closed temporarily on April 18, 1895, the Carson City Mint would never again coin money, and superintendent Jewett W. Adams was required to open an "Embezzlement Account" to replace the losses. The Treasury Department did, however, permit the Carson City Mint to reopen again in June of 1896 as an assay office to refine bullion into ingots. Congress formally conferred the reduction in status on the mint in 1899, and in August, 22 tons of CC silver dollars (approximately 750,000 of them) were removed from the mint and shipped by train to the East Coast, where they remained in storage until the 1960s. All the coining equipment was disassembled and shipped to other facilities.

The Carson City Mint continued to refine the raw gold and silver ore from the mines of Nevada and neighboring states until 1933. In that worst year of the Great Depression, the Carson City Mint was shut down as a cost-cutting measure. With all the employees gone and the doors locked, the future of the historic building may have been an unknown, but what it had accomplished was not in question. From its opening in 1870 until the shutdown of coining operations in 1893, the Carson City Mint had yielded coins with a face value of nearly $50 million. Its beginnings had been plagued with delays and politics; scandals marked its end.

New Role for the Carson City Mint

In 1941, the Carson City Mint building began a new life as the home of the Nevada State Museum. In addition to a display on the history of the Silver State, a walk-through ghost town, a section on Native American culture, and a recreation of an underground mine, the history of the Carson City Mint is told as well.

Of particular interest to coin collectors is a complete assemblage of CC Morgan silver dollars, along with other rare coins struck at the mint over a century ago. The centerpiece of the numismatic section is a steam-powered press manufactured in Philadelphia: Coin Press No. 1, the press that struck the very first CC-mintmark coin in 1870. In 1955, the press was headed for the scrap heap when a group of businessmen arranged for the State of Nevada to purchase it for $225. Three years later, Coin Press No. 1 was returned to its home in Carson City, where it quickly became one of the museum's favorite attractions.

THE GENERAL SERVICES ADMINISTRATION AND CC DOLLARS

Hundreds of millions of Morgan dollars were minted between 1878 and 1904 and in 1921; the fact that rarities exist is mostly a function of large-scale meltings over the years.

Most of the rarer branch-mint issues and apparently all 12,000 of the 1895 Philadelphia circulation strikes were lost to melting. In all, 333,022,048 silver dollars were melted from 1883 to 1964, which represented almost half of the Morgan dollars and possibly 75% of the Peace dollars ever struck. The Pittman Act of 1918 mandated about 81% of these meltings. With the paper dollar becoming more popular for commerce, dollar coins vanished from circulation and piled up in bank vaults. More meltings (approximately 52 million coins) were required by the War Time Silver Act of 1942. Then, in 1979 and 1980, when silver shot up to nearly $50 per ounce, no doubt even more millions of Morgans and Peace dollars were melted. Today, it is estimated that only 15% to 17% of all Morgan dollars produced still exist.

The finest of the Carson City Proofs of any denomination: this 1893-CC coin, graded PF-67 and pedigreed to the famous Jack Lee collection

Even as the numismatic hobby underwent rapid growth beginning in the 1930s, interest in other collecting areas far outpaced the attention paid to the large Morgan "cartwheels." Most collectors preferred the lower-face-value coins (with their lower cost) that were readily available in circulation. Although it was possible to order silver dollars through banks or directly from the Treasury, few noticed or cared. In the late 1930s, however, several Washington dealers learned that the Treasury Department's Cash Room near the White House was paying out uncirculated Carson City dollar coins having a market value of $5 or more at the time! More than a few dealers quietly exploited this discovery throughout the 1940s and 1950s.

In the early 1960s, with silver rising in price, opportunists recognized the chance to turn fast profits by redeeming Silver Certificates for dollar coins (mostly Morgans) at the Treasury. By the time the government closed this lucrative window in 1964, only 2.9 million cartwheels were left in its vaults, almost all of them scarce Carson City Morgans. These were dispersed by the General Services Administration in a series of mail-bid sales from 1972 through 1980, earning big profits for the government and triggering great new interest in silver dollars.

The Public Finally Appreciates the Morgan Dollar

The story of the Morgan silver dollar is a Cinderella tale if there ever was one. Largely ignored by the public since its inception in 1878, in January of 1960 a staggering 180 million silver dollars still remained in Treasury vaults. Today, Morgan dollars are among the most widely pursued and collected of all U.S. coins.

Major key date-and-mintmark combinations include 1895, 1893-S, 1895-O, 1892-S, 1884-S, 1879-CC, and 1889-CC. Mint records show that 12,000 circulation-strike dollars were made in Philadelphia in 1895, but only the 880 Proofs of that year are presently known. Proofs were made for every year in the series, but only a few brilliant Proofs — variously reported as numbering 15 to 24 — are known for 1921. The most exciting surviving Proofs are those minted by the branch mints; of these, several years exist from the Carson City Mint. The 1883-CC, 1884-CC, and 1893-CC would be considered cornerstones of any great silver-dollar collection and can capture several hundred thousand dollars when seen. Prooflike and deep mirror prooflike Morgan dollars from the Carson City Mint found in GSA holders are truly scarce in all dates and are highly prized by collectors.

A Feeding Frenzy Quickly Develops

It was in the early 1960s that word leaked out that some ultra-rare dates were being found in the bags of coins being distributed at face value to the public. A feeding frenzy quickly ensued, with long lines of coin collectors and dealers seeking unopened $1,000 bags of silver dollars. John Q. Public was instantly transformed into a coin speculator, in what must have seemed like a giant government give-away. The numismatic world was about to change.

Prior to the Treasury release of bags of silver dollars, the 1903-O was so rare that it enjoyed the moniker "King of Morgan Dollars." In fact, the 1962 Guide Book of United States Coins (popularly known as the Red Book), which listed the collector value of all

Morgan dollars, had the 1903-O in Uncirculated condition at $1,500. Compare this to an 1893-S which in the same grade was worth considerably less!

All of a sudden, everyone wanted silver dollars! Remember the 180 million coins the government held in early 1960? By January 1964 the hoard had shrunk to only 28 million. The government eventually realized the reason for this rampant speculation, and it halted the public distribution of the Treasury hoard in late March of that year. An audit was then taken of the remaining dollars.

Procedures to Sell the CC Dollar Hoard

But there were still more surprises. Of the remaining 28 million coins, it turned out that 2.9 million were CC dollars—those rare silver dollars struck at the Carson City branch mint from 1878 to 1893. Naturally, this touched off an even greater powder keg of excitement in the collecting community. The question for government officials was how to distribute these very special coins in such a way that everyone who wanted one would have an equal opportunity to get one.

After studying a number of possible approaches, the Congressional Joint Committee on Coinage proposed a series of mail-bid sales as the fairest solution, and the idea was finally enacted into law in December of 1970. Who would handle the sale? After further discussion, the General Services Administration was chosen for the task, and in July 1971, $10 million was set aside for the GSA to develop the necessary plans and procedures to sell the CC dollar hoard.

A multi-stage process was developed that began with inspection of the coins, followed by a determination of their state of preservation, and finally, their being sorted by quality. On the administrative side, staffing requirements would need to be settled, ordering procedures developed, and other parts of the process would need to be finalized. Packaging would be a key factor, and an entire advertising campaign would need to be developed to ensure that the government maximized its revenues. All in all, this was a tall order for the GSA to undertake—and after the smoke had cleared, reviews of its performance were mixed at best.

The first order of business was to move the 2.9 million silver dollars from the original location at the Treasury Department to the West Point Bullion Depository in New York. Care to guess what 3 million silver dollars weigh? According to noted authority Leroy Van Allen, 77 tons is a rough approximation, and it took seven semi-trailer trucks under heavy guard to make the transfer to West Point in January 1970.

The "A" Team

While plans were still forming, a team of well-known American numismatists was assembled in March of 1972 to set the standards for determining the state of preservation of the coins in the Treasury's possession. This was important, since it was recognized that the value of each silver dollar was dependent upon its condition. Members of the team included such luminaries as Amon Carter, John J. Pittman, Henry Grunt Hal, Cliff Mahler, and Margo Russell. This "A" team was given the rather daunting task of creating grading guidelines, with the goal that the coins would later be sorted based on the standards the team developed.

John J. Pittman   Amon Carter

The plan was simple. Select fifty coins from the Treasury Hoard and divide them into two groups: those that met the team's criteria for unimpaired, Uncirculated condition and those that didn't. The people who'd be tasked with sorting the huge hoard of silver dollars would later use these reference coins as their standards. Although it would have been preferable to have a mechanized approach to sorting, such technology was not available. The result was that a small group of heavily supervised individuals were employed to hand-sort the entire 2.9 million coins.

The first step was to divide up the entire hoard according to the date and mintmark of each coin. These sorted silver dollars were then placed in one of three classes: The first consisted of all the coins that met the standard for "Uncirculated." The second included the coins that were deemed inferior, due to minor scratching or toned coloring. The third class contained all the rest of the hoard that was deemed excessively scratched, gouged, or abraded. Fascinating to us now, all the minting errors in the hoard, such as off-centers and the like, were placed in the "reject" category. The value of these today is staggering!

Leroy Van Allen, in what's known as "the VAM book," describes the rest of the process this way: "As the coins were sorted they were placed into special wooden boxes with sliding Masonite tops. Tolerances of the boxes were such that not one coin more than fifty stacks of twenty coins could fit into a box. Each box of a thousand had a seal that was recorded in the log book. This sorting operation took most of what remained of 1972."

Let the Sales Begin!

A total of seven GSA dollar sales were conducted beginning in October 1972. This first distribution of coins focused on the three most common Carson City dates—the

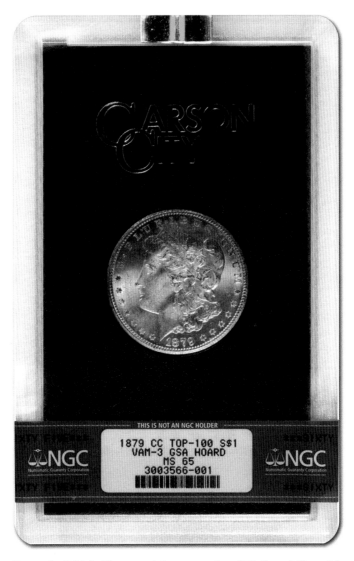

Front of a GSA holder containing a rare 1879-CC silver dollar, with an NGC label certifying the coin as a VAM 3 "Capped Die" variety

1882-CC, the 1883-CC, and the 1884-CC—and all were priced at $30 each. This pricing was only marginally below their market price at the time, and although more than 800 thousand silver dollars found new owners, the event was not a sell-out.

Then, in June of 1973, the same three dates were offered again, along with the entire supply of 1878-CC, 1890-CC, and 1891-CC dollars. Also included were coins from the "Mixed CC," "Mixed Uncirculated," and "Mixed Circulated" subcategories.

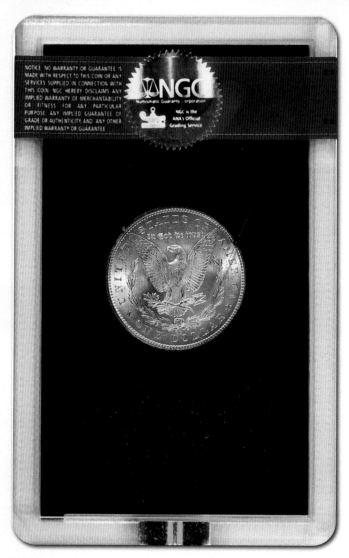

Back of the GSA holder on the previous page

The third sale, which began in October of 1973, contained only three dates, the 1880-CC, 1881-CC, and 1885-CC. More than 200,000 coins were sold.

February 1974 saw the fourth sale focus strictly on the 3,600 or so 1879-CC coins from the hoard. The minimum bid was $300, and prices for the entire GSA holding were bid up to an average of $478.39 per coin. Not surprisingly, the auction was a sell-out. Needless to say, there would be a lot of takers at this price today!

Typical silver mining scene, late 1880s.

THE CARSON CITY SILVER DOLLARS
THE LAST OF A LEGACY

Cover of a brochure issued by the GSA to individuals interested in bidding on pieces from the government hoard of Carson City silver dollars

Over $400,000 in Coins Found in Nevada Basement

The publicity surrounding the 1974 discovery of coins in the basement of the Nevada home of eccentric LaVere Redfield dramatically increased the interest in Morgans. After word leaked out of the amazing cache, valued at more than $400,000, several dealers got into the act, each jockeying for position in a scramble that ultimately ended with a Probate Court auction held in January of 1976. At that sale, A-Mark Coins of Los Angeles captured the hoard with a winning bid of $7.3 million. The coins were cooperatively marketed by a number of dealers over a period of several years. Rather than depressing prices, the orderly dispersal of these coins only served to bring more collectors into the Morgan dollar fold. Similarly, the early 1980s witnessed the equally successful distribution of the 1.5 million silver dollars in the Continental Bank hoard.

The Redfield find got a lot of publicity, and as the U.S. population had become a great deal more familiar with the value of its silver coins in the years following the change from silver coinage to clad, the Morgan dollar finally came into its own as a popular collectible series. The publication of the *Comprehensive Catalog and Encyclopedia of Peace and Morgan Silver Dollars* (the VAM book), by Leroy Van Allen and George Mallis, also spurred significant collector interest in Morgans.

Following closely on the heels of the February sale, another auction was undertaken in April of 1974. All the leftover coins dated 1880-CC through 1885-CC were offered, along with slightly more than 200,000 coins from the "Mixed CC" category. The supply of 1882-CC coins sold out, but the market was growing saturated from what appeared to be constant GSA sales.

Taking this declining demand into account, the GSA was forced to consider altering its original marketing plan. But in order to do so, the original legislation of 1970 had to be amended. Now, armed with a new law in March of 1979, the GSA came up with an alternate approach to sell the remaining 1883-CC and 1884-CC coins. The 1883-CCs would sell for $42 each and the 1884-CCs could be obtained for only $40. To sweeten the pot, all the coins in the "Mixed CC" category would be sold for only $20 each. The only limitation was that the buyer, at least initially, was limited to ordering a total of 500 coins from each category.

As we all know, the best-laid plans of mice and men can easily go astray. The problem here was the escalating price of silver. For those of us who can remember the heady days of late 1979 and early 1980, when the spot price of silver went from less than $10 per troy ounce to an intra-day high of $50 per ounce, the GSA found itself in a difficult situation. The silver content of the coins to be sold in the "Mixed CC" category at $20 contained almost $30 in silver!

It was decided that the best way out was to change to a flexible pricing structure for the CC dollars in the sixth GSA sale. On the date of the sale, prospective buyers were asked to call a toll-free number that would provide final pricing information for the three categories of coins available. It ended up that the 1883-CC was $65, the 1884-CC was $60, and the "Mixed CC" coins were $45 each. As might be expected, the skyrocketing silver prices added an element of speculation to purchasing these hundred-year-old cartwheels, and ordering limits were imposed. But even with this confusion, more than 900,000 Carson City dollars were dispersed to the public in the final GSA sale.

How successful were these sales? A Congressional committee that looked into the GSA operations encountered a veritable mountain of complaints. But in hindsight, it was an amazing venture involving the government of the United States and its citizens. Certainly, it was a long process from the time the government became aware of the 2.9 million historically important Carson City silver dollars in its possession in 1964, to the concluding GSA sales in 1980. And government procedures were often clumsy and inadequate. But, measured another way, these sales provided total receipts approaching $100 million to be funneled into government coffers. In that sense at least, the GSA sales were a resounding success.

But more than that, this grand distribution of scarce and desirable coins has allowed countless collectors to hold a piece of Wild West history in their hands. As for today, CC dollars in GSA cases are one of the hottest areas of numismatics. As the echoes of complaints about the details of the GSA sales die away, what remains is the mystique of the Comstock Lode and the silver dollars made famous by "Silver Dick" Bland and the Mint at Carson City. These CC dollars will preserve this legacy for centuries to come!

A circulated Carson City Morgan dollar in its GSA packaging

2

HOW TO COLLECT CARSON CITY MORGAN SILVER DOLLARS

Without question, the Morgan silver dollar has become one of the most popular U.S. coin series since the release of the GSA hoard beginning in 1972. While they are not the rarest coins on the market, Carson City mintmarks are among the most popular with collectors and investors alike. With the release of the GSA hoard, the collecting community was exposed to thousands of high-grade examples and many previously unknown die varieties, and many more are probably waiting to be discovered. Each coin brings to life the imagination of the Wild West, the Comstock Lode discovery, and the pioneering spirit of a young nation in which hundreds of thousands went in search of their dreams. Clearly, coinage with a CC mintmark has a bright future, as the number of collectors, hoarders, and investors continues to grow.

This is the first book written specifically on the GSA Carson City silver dollar hoard and the many varieties found in each year of mintage. We hope this reference will continue to inspire the demand created more than 40 years ago, when the release of these exciting and affordable coins was announced. Nothing like the "coin-a-mania" created by the GSA sales had ever happened, nor will probably ever happen again.

We believe there is a tremendous need for a book dedicated to specific collector needs regarding the Carson City Morgan dollar series, because of the surge in collectors and investors prompted by the Internet. Certainly the abundance of price and historical information makes the buying, selling, trading, and holding of these coins more appealing. As the demand for ownership grows, so does the need for information, and the goal of this book is to make this asset class fun to own, as opposed to just looking at numbers on a statement.

Rare coins—particularly those that are historically exciting—have an intellectual appeal. As we grow older (and, hopefully, wiser and richer), we tend to take more interest in history, and these little round works of art and human ingenuity become a stimulus for historical research—especially of financial history, which can enhance our knowledge of other asset classes. This knowledge will make any of us a wiser and richer investor.

Carson City Morgan silver dollars are desirable for a variety of reasons. They are among the biggest and most beautifully designed of all U.S. coins. They were struck during an extraordinary historic era (1878–1893) and have wonderful stories to tell. Many issues are sufficiently available that they can be found in high grades, making them aesthetically pleasing for a very modest investment. Yet there also are a number of truly rare dates, especially in high grades, that appeal to the advanced collector.

There are a number of ways to collect Carson City Morgan silver dollars, and the following are a few we suggest.

COLLECTING CARSON CITY MORGAN DOLLARS AS TYPE COINS

Type-coin collectors try to find representative examples of specific types or designs. For Morgan silver dollars, a type collector would most likely focus on issues such as the 1882-CC, 1883-CC, or 1884-CC from the GSA hoard. Beautiful examples are available in MS-65 condition and, although much harder to locate, can be found as high as MS-66.

A type set could be made more interesting by including a date from the 1870s, the 1880s, and the 1890s—the three decades in which silver dollars were minted in Carson City. The most common issue from the 1870s is the 1878-CC; for the 1880s it's the 1884-CC; and for the 1890s, the 1891-CC. All these dates can be found in grades high enough to satisfy even the most discriminating collector, although the 1891-CC is quite challenging in grades above MS-63. The 1878-CC would be the logical choice if one is looking for a single piece for a type set. It is not only the first Carson City Morgan dollar, it is the first year of the series as well. The first year of any new coin is sought by many thousands of first-year type collectors, providing substantial support for prices and adding a high degree of liquidity. With patience these dates can be found with exceptional aesthetic eye appeal in choice grades; however, as with all Morgan dollars, it is worth paying a premium at each grade level in order to acquire beautiful coins.

COLLECTING ALL CARSON CITY MORGAN DOLLARS BY DATE AND MINTMARK ONLY

The Morgan silver dollar was produced at five mints: Philadelphia, New Orleans, San Francisco, Carson City, and Denver. Some collectors take on the major challenge of attempting to assemble a complete set of Morgan dollars from every year and mint, while others find it more interesting to collect issues from only one mint. Of all the mintages, only Carson City, comprising 13 different dates, conjures in the imagination images of the Wild West and the major silver strike of the Comstock Lode.

Collecting only the Carson City Mint issue provides an interesting (and next to impossible) challenge for the collector focusing specifically on coins encased within GSA holders. That's because the 1889-CC, 1892-CC, and 1893-CC are currently known to have only one example each in a GSA holder. The 1889-CC has been seen by the authors; however, the 1892-CC and 1893-CC are only believed to exist, though credible sources do confirm their existence. Recently we had the pleasure of viewing the 1889-CC encased in a GSA black holder after its recent certification by the Numismatic Guaranty Corporation of America (NGC) as MS-62PL. For most collectors seeking to complete a date

Selby Ungar (left) and Adam Crum with the GSA-encased 1889-CC dollar pictured on the following page

and CC mintmark set of Morgan silver dollars, these dates most likely will not be GSA encased.

A complete date set, excluding varieties, of Carson City Morgan silver dollars in Choice Uncirculated condition, with every piece (except for 1889, 1892, and 1893) in a GSA holder, could fetch up to $75,000 depending on the collector's desire for eye appeal or beautiful toning. Up to two-thirds of the set's cost would be due to the 1889-CC. In Gem condition, the same set could be a lifelong challenge to achieve and carry costs of up to three-quarters of a million dollars or more, again depending on the collector's desire for quality and attractive toning. For the collector who wants simply to find nice coins, like Choice Uncircu-

The only 1889-CC Morgan silver dollar that is known to exist in a GSA holder (see p. 103 for a full image)

lated for common dates and About Uncirculated to appealing Uncirculated for the tougher dates, set costs could be limited to fit almost any collector's budget.

COLLECTING ALL CARSON CITY MORGAN DOLLARS BY DATE AND VAM VARIETY

If you are excited enough about Carson City Morgan silver dollars to read this book, you may want to join the growing numbers of collectors who have assumed the challenge of collecting all the years and dies known as VAM varieties. The term "VAM" comes from two numismatists who collected Morgan dollars and, through studying different coins, began to notice slight differences from one coin to another. Leroy Van Allen and George Mallis started taking notes and cataloging the different die varieties. Their numbering system has become known by the acronym of their last names: VAM varieties. Over the years, collecting these varieties has become a popular way to collect Carson City Morgans and has made it more challenging and fulfilling to the serious collector. It has put a true meaning to the cliché "enjoying the hunt" for thousands of Morgan dollar collectors. The key to collecting, both by year and VAM variety, is to obtain one example of each year and one of each important VAM variety within each year. There are dozens of known VAM varieties and certainly more to be discovered. This aspect should make the hunt even more interesting; instead of collecting only 13 examples by year, the collector will discover that collecting different VAMs can provide years of enjoyment.

In such a set, it is advisable to select the most affordable, but eye-appealing, coin. If a higher-quality coin presents itself and the time is right, then an upgrade may be in order. But for the purposes of collecting the tougher VAM varieties, it may be advisable to take what one can get in regards to technical grade, without settling for an aesthetically under-appealing coin.

A complete year-and-VAM-variety set may never be achieved, because there are sure to be more VAM varieties discovered, but only through the pursuit of such a goal will these discoveries be possible. The investment required for such a set would be difficult to calculate because of many factors, not the least of which is the collector's desire for aesthetics.

There are some practical guidelines that collectors assembling complete sets should follow. A set should be as well-matched as possible; the collector should try to purchase coins that are relatively similar in appearance. As an example, the collector might try to acquire pieces that are as original as possible and have reasonably similar coloration.

A complete set should not be "all over the map" as far as grades are concerned. It makes no sense to assemble a set that has lower About Uncirculated coins alongside pieces that grade MS-65. It is advisable to use common sense when filling in the holes and try to match grades as closely as possible.

Do not attempt to assemble a complete set with unrealistic expectations. A collector who has assembled more common sets may approach Carson City Morgan silver dollars with the goal of completing this set in higher grades. However, since a number of the tougher dates are difficult to locate in MS-65, the collector needs to learn what is realistic for each issue. For example, it is unrealistic to expect to find the 1889-CC in a GSA holder, much less in MS-65; but it *is* realistic to seek an 1884-CC in this grade level (or even higher) and in a GSA holder. See table 1 for a comparison of regular-issue rarities.

In Choice Uncirculated grades, a complete set of Carson City Morgan silver dollars, including the many different VAM varieties, would carry investment costs in excess of $100,000 at the time of this writing.

Many numismatists believe that building a set is a good way to realize additional value without spending extra money. This phenomenon is known as a "set premium" and clearly applies to Morgan silver dollars. Carefully assembled sets of coins have proven to bring strong premiums over random, meaningless accumulations. A set intelligently assembled by a shrewd collector with the assistance of a professional numismatist generally proves to be emotionally—and financially—rewarding to that collector.

Whatever your specific goals, the most important thing to remember in assembling a set is to collect what you enjoy. The "thrill of the hunt" is the primary motivation, and the knowledge you gain will make collecting these fascinating Carson City silver dollars that much more satisfying.

Table 1. Carson City Morgan Dollars: Rarity Rankings

GSA			Non-GSA	
Rank	Year	Total Holdings	Rank	Year
1st	1889-CC	1	1st	1889-CC
	1892-CC	1	2nd	1893-CC
	1893-CC	1	3rd	1892-CC
4th	1890-CC	3,949	4th	1891-CC
5th	1879-CC	4,123	5th	1879-CC
6th	1891-CC	5,687	6th	1890-CC
7th	1878-CC	60,993	7th	1878-CC
8th	1880-CC	131,529	8th	1880-CC
9th	1881-CC	147,485	9th	1885-CC
10th	1885-CC	148,285	10th	1882-CC
11th	1882-CC	605,029	11th	1884-CC
12th	1883-CC	755,518	12th	1881-CC
13th	1884-CC	962,638	13th	1883-CC

3

CARSON CITY MORGAN SILVER DOLLARS: ALL DATES, PLUS SELECTED VARIETIES

This chapter presents the Carson City Morgan dollars in a standardized format: first, the "generic" issue for each date, then the most popular of its known VAM varieties—in all, 29 different dates and selections. Certainly there are more VAM varieties to be discovered in GSA holders, which was, in fact, one of the goals that inspired this book.

Where possible, each entry is generously illustrated: in a GSA holder (if such is known to exist); enlarged and actual-size obverse and reverse photos; and super-enlargements of important details. Many of the coins shown are among the highest-quality specimens in the world, and were chosen not to make you feel that a lower-grade coin is "inferior" or not worth owning, but to inspire you, to fire your enthusiasm for collecting!

Each entry has a chart of estimated values in specified Mint State grades, listing prooflike (PL) and deep-mirror prooflike (DMPL) values—the epitome of value-added features—separately. A dash indicates that a coin is too rare to price in that grade, while a blank indicates it is not known to exist in that grade. Each generic listing has a "By the Numbers" chart, which gives its original mintage, Leroy Van Allen's published estimate of the number in the GSA hoard, rarity rankings for GSA and non-GSA examples, and other useful facts. "Overall Rarity" is the total number of coins estimated to exist for an issue, based on the number found in the GSA hoard, the number graded by PCGS and NGC, personal observations, "insider" information, auction records, and gut instinct. The estimates are most likely accurate for the rarer issues, but may be on the low side for the more common ones.

"Condition Census," for our purposes, refers to the highest reasonable acquisition grade for most collectors. The highest-known grade for a given date might include 10 or more coins—then again, it might include only one or two, with perhaps *dozens* of examples in the next lower grade. To give the huge number of collectors of this popular series a reasonable goal, we put as the target grade the top 50 or so coins and called it the condition census. Though it isn't always possible to acquire the highest-graded coins in GSA holders, it's still desirable, and fun, to attempt to do so.

"Collector Insights" give summaries of useful background information on each entry, while "Variety Notes" supply valuable information on the many die (VAM) varieties known to exist for Carson City Morgan dollars in GSA holders. For a more challenging approach to the entire series of Carson City dollars, we recommend adding to your library Leroy Van Allen and George Mallis's *Comprehensive Catalog of Morgan and Peace Silver Dollars*, along with Jeff Oxman and Michael Fey's *The Top 100 Morgan Dollar Varieties: The VAM Keys.*

1878-CC
(GENERIC)

1878-CC dollars in GSA holders enjoy a special appeal, not only because they are first-year issues, but also because they are rare in high grades.

Valuations

		GSA	MS-61	MS-62	MS-63	MS-64	MS-65	MS-66	MS-67
In GSA Case	MS	$600	$650	$675	$800	$1,300	$6,750	$18,000	
(Graded by NGC)	PL	700	750	850	1,100	3,000	17,000	25,000	
	DMPL	800	1,250	1,750	2,500	17,500			
Slabbed	MS		275	400	500	675	1,900	6,000	$37,500
(Not in GSA Case)	PL		275	500	600	1100	2,700	8,000	
	DMPL		325	750	2,000	3,100	9,600	30,000	

There are two types of reverse on 1878-CC specimens. The earlier type has what is called a "B[1] reverse," which simply means the center arrow shaft at the feather end of the arrows is longer than on the later type, where it is flush with the inside feathers. Why is this important? VAMs 6, 18, and 24, which are the key ultra-rarities of the date, all have the B[1]-type reverse.

By the Numbers

Original Mintage	2,212,000
Total GSA Holdings	60,993
Percentage of Mintage in GSA	2.70%
Original Uncirculated Designation	47,567
Not Designated Due to Scratches/Toning etc.	13,426
GSA Overall Rarity Ranking	7th
Non-GSA Rarity Ranking	7th
GSA Prooflike or DMPL Availability	Very Rare

Condition Census

In GSA Case	MS-65
PCGS or NGC	MS-67

1878-CC (generic)

Collector Insights

Representing the first year of Morgan dollar production, the 1878-CC is surprisingly hard to find in a GSA hard case, considering that current estimates of the GSA population are more than 47,000. Add to that another 13,000 specimens in GSA "blue packs" and one would expect the 1878-CC to be readily obtainable. However, it appears that, as a whole, demand for CC dollars has swamped the available supply, and the availability of 1878-CC GSA dollars pales in comparison to the huge supply of 1883-CC and 1884-CC GSA dollars. So the suggestion that the '78-CC is the seventh-hardest CC dollar to find in a GSA holder makes sense. An additional factor sparking collector interest for this date is the discovery that three extremely popular TOP 100 varieties exist in GSA holders: VAMs 11, 18, and 24. One interesting side note to collecting this date is the surprising lack of prooflike and DMPL specimens found in GSA cases. In particular, Deep Mirror Prooflike examples are scarce as hen's teeth, with less than 10 known! Finally, in terms of grades, a quick glance at the Condition Census table makes it clear that MS-65 is basically the top end for coins in a GSA holder. Yet keep in mind that NGC has already graded a total of 77 in that grade, so it might be considered prudent not to settle for anything less than a high-end, certified example.

Variety Notes

There are more than 25 varieties known for the 1878-CC, of which only four are featured in the TOP 100 VAM book. Interestingly, three of these, VAMs 6, 18, and 24, display some of the best doubled-die obverses in the Morgan dollar series, with spectacular doubling on the leaves and cotton bolls adorning Liberty's bonnet. The numerals of the date, as well as other obverse features, also show strong doubling on these varieties. It can also be helpful for attribution purposes to note that all three have a B1 Reverse, characterized by a long center shaft on the arrows held in the eagle's talons. In any case, it's worth remembering that of the three, only the VAM 18 and VAM 24 have thus far been found in GSA holders. Want fame and fortune? Find an 1878-CC VAM 6 in a GSA case!

1878-CC VAM 6

Collector Insights

The purpose of this GSA Carson City dollar guide is not only to discuss what is presently known about GSA-encapsulated Morgan dollars, but also to recommend what to look for in the way of new discoveries. So, armed with the information given here, the reader is encouraged to check the GSA cases he or she already owns to see if any are the 1878-CC VAM 6 variety. Up to this point, no VAM 6 specimens have come to light, but that is not to say none exists. It is heartening to note that a limited number of another 1878-CC variety, the VAM 18 (which shares the same doubled-die obverse as the VAM 6), *is* known in GSA holders. And those VAM 18 specimens that have recently entered the numismatic marketplace have brought tremendous premiums for their lucky owners. Clearly, it makes sense to acquire any 1878-CC specimen in a GSA holder that displays strong doubling on Liberty's headdress. And if the CC mintmark touches the right wreath on the lower reverse, you've just made a new discovery that might be the highlight of your numismatic career!

Variety Notes

The VAM 6 is a rare variety that hasn't turned up in a GSA case yet, so finding one is a high priority for large numbers of specialists. Here is what to look for to identify the VAM 6: Both VAMs 6 and 18 have the same obverse, with its dramatic doubling of the right edges of the leaves and cotton bolls in Liberty's bonnet, but to distinguish the VAM 6 from the VAM 18, simply examine the placement of the "CC" mintmark on the reverse. If the right C touches the wreath above it, you have a VAM 6; if both Cs are centered under the ribbon bow and neither approaches the wreath, you have a VAM 18. Looking for a pot of gold at the end of the rainbow? Find an 1878-CC VAM 6 in a GSA case.

1878-CC VAM 11

Spectacular die features are the lifeblood of
variety collectors, and VAM 11 displays some
extraordinary gouges on the eagle's wings.

Valuations		GSA	MS-61	MS-62	MS-63	MS-64	MS-65
In GSA Case	MS	$650	$750	$950	$1,200	$1,650	$17,000
(Graded by NGC)	PL	800	900	1,150	1,600	3,000	
	DMPL	900	1,400	2,500	5,000	20,000	
Slabbed	MS		300	400	500	700	2,300
(Not in GSA Case)	PL		500	600	700	900	2,800
	DMPL		750	850	2,200	3,500	12,500

The unusual die gouges at the bottom of the eagle's right wing (viewer's left) are the key diagnostics for this variety. However, there are die gouges in the eagle's left wing as well, which variety collectors have generally ignored.

Condition Census

In GSA Case	MS-64
PCGS or NGC	MS-65

1878-CC, VAM 11

Collector Insights

Because the Bland-Allison Coinage Act of 1878 mandated the striking of $2 million worth of bullion into silver dollars on a monthly basis, officials at the Philadelphia Mint looked westward to the Carson City and San Francisco branch mints to help meet this huge production quota. The necessary dies arrived in Carson City on April 16, 1878, and the coin presses were striking silver dollars the next day. It's thought that the first dies to arrive in Carson City had a reverse design known as the "long-nock B^1 reverse" (the nock being the end of an arrow shaft that connects with an archer's bow string). VAM 11 has a B^2 reverse characterized by a "short nock," the primary reverse type used for the rest of 1878. In terms of availability, the VAM 11 doesn't take years of searching to find a specimen, unlike the VAM 18, which is rarely, if ever, encountered. This is not to say the VAM 11 is common, but rather collectors celebrate the fact that it is obtainable both in GSA hard cases and in GSA "blue envelope" soft packs, with at least 50 pieces of the former and 25 of the latter known to the authors.

Variety Notes

The VAM 11, available both inside and out of GSA holders, is a unique die variety, and its widespread appeal landed it in the original TOP 100 Morgan dollar variety listings. VAM 11 features bold, crisscrossing lines on the eagle's wings, and the effect is dramatic. In particular, the eagle's lower right wing (viewer's left) shows a pattern of intersecting lines that at first appear part of the actual wing design. No one has been able to explain the nature of these raised die-polishing lines, other than to speculate that an engraver made them by accident while preparing the die. Indeed, it may be the case that, in the eyes of 19th-century Mint employees, such die-preparation errors were not considered important. After all, who would look that closely? But fast-forward more than 125 years, and today's variety specialists, armed with 15-power loupes and 30-power microscopes, are greatly intrigued by such dramatic engraving errors.

1878-CC
VAM 18

The 1878-CC VAM 18, whether inside or outside a GSA slab, is normally found with PL or DMPL surfaces in grades ranging from MS-60 to MS-62.

Valuations		GSA	MS-61	MS-62	MS-63
In GSA Case	MS				
(Graded by NGC)	PL	$7,500	$10,000		
	DMPL				
Slabbed	MS		2,000	$4,000	$7,000
(Not in GSA Case)	PL				
	DMPL				

One of the telltale VAM 18 features is doubling on the right side of the numerals of the date.

The strong doubling on the leaves and cotton bolls on VAM 18 gives this variety its name, Doubled Obverse.

Dramatic doubling is evident up and down the entire back edge of Liberty's ear on this variety.

This mintmark is distinctive, with the CC centered below the ribbon bow, and not touching the wreath.

Condition Census

In GSA Case	MS-61
PCGS or NGC	MS-61

1878-CC VAM 18

Collector Insights

Up to this point, only six 1878-CC, VAM 18 specimens have been found in GSA cases, making the variety exceedingly desirable to collectors. It has been reported that an MS-61 Prooflike VAM 18 in a GSA holder sold for $2,500 in early 2006; when another GSA MS-61 PL specimen entered the marketplace a few months later, exuberant bidding pushed the price up to $3,000. As of this writing, at least one more VAM 18 in a GSA case is known that hasn't been graded by NGC, and there are probably more. For attribution purposes, the key to identifying the VAM 18 is to confirm strong doubling on the obverse design features of Liberty's bonnet, and then to look at the lower reverse. Unlike the VAM 6, on which the right C of the CC mintmark touches the base of the right wreath, the VAM 18 mintmark is centered under the ribbon bow, and neither C touches the wreath. Outside GSA holders, slabbed VAM 18 specimens are extremely rare and popular, but the real variety superstar is the specimen inside a GSA case.

Variety Notes

This Carson City variety, together with its VAM 6 counterpart, is a key component of any TOP 100 variety set of Morgan dollars. Both VAMs show the same strong doubling on the obverse, including clearly defined doubled leaves in Liberty's headdress. Liberty's ear is also doubled, as is the date. The problem here is not identifying this variety, it's finding one! Outside a GSA case, the VAM 18 is sought-after in all grades and most often encountered in lower Mint State condition with Prooflike surfaces. This fact is reflected in its "Pivotal Grade" rating of only MS-62 outside a GSA case and MS-61 in one. What this tells us is that, above the MS-61/62 range, a VAM 18 in a GSA hard plastic holder would be worth a king's ransom!

1878-CC
VAM 24

The 1878-CC VAM 24 specimen featured in this
photo is unique, as it represents the only example
of this variety in a GSA case to be graded by NGC.

Valuations

		GSA	MS-61
In GSA Case	MS		$13,500
(Graded by NGC)	PL		
	DMPL		
Slabbed	MS		*(1 known)*
(Not in GSA Case)	PL		
	DMPL		

With doubling on the obverse that's similar to that on VAMs 6 and 18, the VAM 24 doubled die is simply spectacular. The shift of the image on the leaves and cotton bolls in Liberty's bonnet is clear and distinct, as is the doubling on the date. All three varieties are extremely rare, but the VAM 24 in a GSA case featured here is one of a kind.

Condition Census

In GSA Case	Unique MS-61
PCGS or NGC	MS-63

1878-CC VAM 24

Collector Insights

It's happened more than once. Just when the numismatic experts conclude that a particular variety doesn't exist, some eagle-eyed collector finds one. That's just what happened with the 1878-CC VAM 24. The authors were prepared to state that no 1878-CC VAM 24 specimens had ever been found in a GSA holder, when the example featured here came to light. Yes, we were a bit skeptical at first, but when we examined the coin, voila! It *was* the legendary VAM 24. Needless to say, even outside a GSA case, the VAM 24 isn't some run-of-the-mill variety, particularly in brilliant Uncirculated condition. Most importantly, what we take away from all this is that thrilling new GSA discoveries are still possible today—the VAM 24 proves it.

Variety Notes

Here's a statistic: of the 2.9 million Carson City silver dollars found in Treasury vaults and ultimately distributed to the public, as of 2014, a total of one 1878-CC VAM 24 has surfaced. Now *that's* rare. And the variety itself is quite interesting. Like VAMs 6 and 18, the VAM 24 has a strongly doubled-die obverse, and as such, is a highly valued TOP 100 variety. But unlike VAMs 6 and 18, the doubling on the VAM 24 obverse does not include Liberty's ear. In fact, all of the doubling is similar, but not exactly the same. So, how can one differentiate between these three premium varieties? First, look at the reverse. Is the CC mintmark centered and not touching the wreath? If so, it's either VAM 18 or 24. Next, look at the obverse. If Liberty's ear shows strong doubling, then you have a VAM 18; if not, you're looking at VAM 24. Hopefully, this simple identification method will help a reader turn up another super-rare VAM 24 specimen!

1879-CC
(GENERIC)

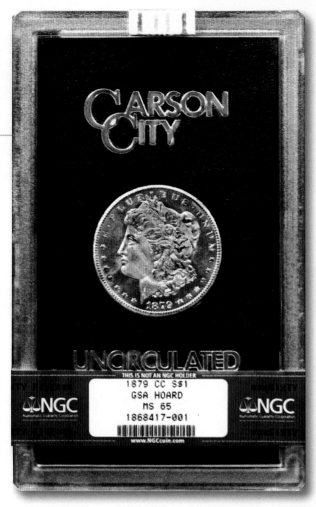

As a date, the 1879-CC is one of the superstars of the Morgan dollar series, and it's even more popular (and expensive!) in a GSA holder.

Valuations

		GSA	MS-61	MS-62	MS-63	MS-64	MS-65
In GSA Case	MS	$7,000	$8,000	$8,750	$10,000	$17,500	$50,000
(Graded by NGC)	PL	8,000	9,750	11,000	16,000	27,000	
	DMPL						
Slabbed	MS		4,500	5,700	7,500	10,500	30,000
(Not in GSA Case)	PL		4,750	6,500	8,500	12,500	32,500
	DMPL		5,000	7,000	13,500	25,000	40,000

In 1879, the small CC-mintmark punch that had
been used in 1878 was replaced by a new punch on
which both Cs in the mintmark were visibly larger.

By the Numbers

Original Mintage	756,000
Total GSA Holdings	4,123
Percentage of Mintage in GSA	0.50%
Original Uncirculated Designation	3,633
Not Designated Due to Scratches/Toning etc.	490
GSA Overall Rarity Ranking	5th
Non-GSA Rarity Ranking	5th
GSA Prooflike or DMPL Availability	Very Rare

Condition Census

In GSA Case	MS-65
PCGS or NGC	MS-66

1879-CC (generic)

Collector Insights

The year 1879 marked the second year of Morgan dollar production at the Carson City branch mint. By this time, silver-dollar design problems at the main Philadelphia Mint had settled down, and only one reverse die type, the so-called C^3 reverse, was used for the entire year. That compares with a multiplicity of reverses employed in 1878, including the 8-TF, the 7/8-TF, the 7-TF with B^1 and B^2 reverses, and the 7-TF with C^1, C^2, and C^3 reverses. Fortunately for today's variety collectors, the 1879-CC reverse dies were not without a significant anomaly. It turns out that one reverse die was apparently left over from the preceding year, of course displaying the small CC mintmark of 1878. The problem? In 1879 the Mint introduce a larger CC that became the standard for the rest of the Morgan dollar series. So, before this reverse die of 1878 could be used in 1879, the original mintmark had to be effaced from the die and the larger mintmark punched over it. As might be expected, some artifacts of the original mintmark remained on the die, resulting in the now-famous Capped Die variety. The upshot is that this is the only confirmed Morgan dollar "Large Over Small Mintmark" variety, and it's spectacular!

Variety Notes

The 1879-CC is well known to silver dollar collectors as one of the premier dates in the Morgan dollar series. It's rare and extremely expensive. But for VAM collectors, it is also noteworthy for one unique mintmark variety. By way of background, all mintmarks were applied to the dies at the Philadelphia Mint, where they were also repunched into the die to strengthen the image or to correct the mintmark's position. But, as explained above, in the case of one 1879-CC reverse a leftover die from 1878 was made usable by removing the smaller mintmark and replacing it with a larger CC mintmark. The unanticipated result was that artifacts from the first mintmark remained, creating what is now called the Capped Die variety. How important is it? The 1879-CC VAM 3 is one of the few Morgan dollar varieties listed in just about every pricing guide, including those for non-variety collectors.

1879-CC
VAM 3

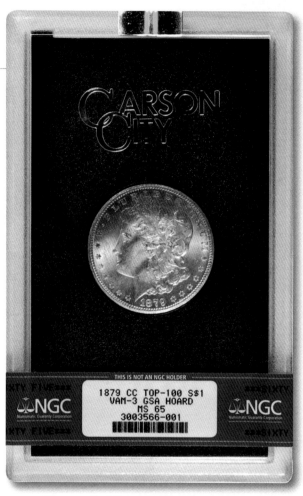

THIS IS NOT AN NGC HOLDER

1879 CC TOP-100 S$1
VAM-3 GSA HOARD
MS 65
3003566-001

NGC
Numismatic Guaranty Corporation

NGC
Numismatic Guaranty Corporation

The so-called Capped Die variety was once
thought of as a "poor man's" 1879-CC, but now
is recognized as a major rarity in its own right,
particularly in high grades with PL or DMPL surfaces.

Valuations

		GSA	MS-61	MS-62	MS-63	MS-64	MS-65
In GSA Case	MS	$7,000	$8,000	$8,750	$11,000	$22,000	$70,000
(Graded by NGC)	PL						
	DMPL						
Slabbed	MS		4,500	5,750	6,750	11,000	40,000
(Not in GSA Case)	PL		4,500	5,750	8,000	13,500	50,000
	DMPL		5,000	7,500	12,500	50,000	70,000

On the 1879-CC Capped Die obverse,
the first two numerals are doubled at the top
outside; this is especially evident on the 1.

On the Capped Die variety, the area surrounding the
Carson City mintmark displays the partially effaced
remains of an underlying small CC mintmark.

Condition Census

In GSA Case	MS-64
PCGS or NGC	MS-65

1879-CC VAM 3

Collector Insights

The 1879-CC "Capped Die" variety is an anomaly in the Morgan dollar series in that the mintmark is actually a Large Over Small CC mintmark. In recent years, its popularity has continued to grow, even though the VAM 3 is no rarer than its non-variety counterpart in grades below gem brilliant Uncirculated. However, this situation turns around in the MS-65, MS-66, and MS-67 grades, where prices for top-end "Capped Die" specimens overtake their non-variety counterparts. The fact that NGC has slabbed more than 500 VAM 3 examples, of which only six are MS-65 or above, paints a clear picture of this rarity in high grades. Also worth noting is the fact that prooflike and deep mirror prooflike Capped Die specimens may be quite undervalued, considering how infrequently they're encountered. This is particularly true for the VAM 3 in GSA government holders, since NGC has not graded a single prooflike or deep mirror prooflike specimen in a GSA case higher than MS-64. As for rarity in GSA cases, only two specimens have surfaced in a GSA holder that NGC has graded MS-65. No wonder the ever-popular 1879-CC is considered such an extraordinary date with GSA specialists.

Variety Notes

Of the fewer than six known die pairs used at the Carson City Mint in 1879, only one is of particular interest to collectors: the VAM 3 Capped Die. Actually, the name is a misnomer. The mintmark is not "capped," nor is it "rusted" or "pitted," as is frequently heard. Rather, the raised metal around the VAM 3's mintmark is all that remains of an underlying mintmark that was improperly removed from the die. How did this happen? Coinage dies were so time consuming and costly to produce that Mint personnel naturally tried to rehabilitate unused dies whenever possible. This helps explain why a leftover reverse die from 1878 would be altered and reused in 1879. In the case of the 1879-CC VAM 3, an area of raised metal around the "CC" mintmark is all that remains of the original mintmark of 1878—but it's enough to fire up the imaginations of a virtual army of silver-dollar collectors.

1880-CC
(GENERIC)

Some of the most important overdate varieties in the Morgan dollar series are found on 1880-CC specimens. In fact, it's possible that *all* 1880-CC obverse dies may have been left over from prior years.

Valuations		GSA	MS-61	MS-62	MS-63	MS-64	MS-65	MS-66	MS-67
In GSA Case	MS	$575	$625	$650	$700	$875	$2,000	$7,000	$32,500
(Graded by NGC)	PL	575	650	750	1,000	1,950	7,000	16,000	
	DMPL	800	900	1,500	3,500	10,000	25,000		
Slabbed	MS		550	600	650	800	1,250	2,500	
(Not in GSA Case)	PL		550	625	700	1250	2,000	4,200	23,000
	DMPL		625	700	1,050	2,500	7,950	27,500	42,500

In GSA holders the value of high-grade 1880-CC coins with DMPL
surfaces has skyrocketed to amazing heights in today's market.

By the Numbers

Original Mintage	485,000
Total GSA Holdings	131,529
Percentage of Mintage in GSA	22.10%
Original Uncirculated Designation	114,942
Not Designated Due to Scratches/Toning etc.	16,587
GSA Overall Rarity Ranking	8th
Non-GSA Rarity Ranking	8th
GSA Prooflike or DMPL Availability	Scarce

Condition Census

In GSA Case	MS-66
PCGS or NGC	MS-67

1880-CC (generic)

Collector Insights

For VAM specialists, finding an 1880-CC silver dollar is a like landing on the shores of the Promised Land. Dramatic overdates are everywhere; in fact, most of the spectacular overdates in the Morgan dollar series are 1880-CC. Fortunately for those of us interested in GSA dollars, all three major overdates (VAMs 4, 5, and 6) are well represented in the GSA government hoard of silver dollars. And there is even more to recommend the date: because of the significant numbers of 1880-CC dollars preserved in the GSA hoard, large numbers of high-grade specimens have survived. In fact, outside of GSA cases, eleven 1880-CC MS-67 examples have been graded by NGC, one of which is also prooflike. Even in GSA hard plastic, one MS-67 and eighty-two MS-66 examples are presently known. Most of these, if not all, emerged from the Treasury holdings. A quick perusal of the Condition Census table on the previous page summarizes the availability of this date in high grades.

Variety Notes

Three extraordinary 1880-CC varieties are known to collectors, and each one shows the clear remains of underlying date digits. VAM 4 displays the remains of a 79 under the 80. In the case of VAMs 5 and 6, the visible artifacts inside the loops of the second 8 show an underlying 7. In each case, the resulting overdate features are breathtaking, but even more intriguing is the speculation that all the obverse dies used in Carson City in 1880 originally may have been leftover dies from 1879. Could this be true? It's certainly possible that Mint engravers simply were more successful at removing the original 79 from some dies than from others. With this sense of awe and mystery swirling about the varieties, it's no wonder that VAM enthusiasts and non-variety collectors alike flock to the 1880-CC.

1880-CC
VAM 4
(Reverse of '78)

The 1880-CC VAM 4 overdate is particularly interesting because the remains of an underlying 7 and 9 are so clearly visible inside the last two digits of the date.

Valuations		GSA	MS-61	MS-62	MS-63	MS-64	MS-65	MS-66
In GSA Case	MS	$650	$700	$900	$1,150	$1,600	$5,250	$20,000
(Graded by NGC)	PL	650	825	1,000	1,650	5,500	12,500	
	DMPL	800	1000	1,750	5,000	13,500		
Slabbed	MS		650	900	700	1,150	2,250	6,000
(Not in GSA Case)	PL		650	700	1000	1,750	5,200	
	DMPL		700	1000	2,000	5,000	17,500	

The flat-breast eagle on the VAM 4 reverse is a throwback to the dies originally used in 1878.

For comparison, note the convex shape of the round-breast eagle used on most reverse dies after 1878.

On the VAM 4 date, remains of an underlying 7 and 9 are discernible inside the 8 and 0.

Condition Census

In GSA Case	MS-65
PCGS or NGC	MS-66

1880-CC VAM 4 (Reverse of '78)

Collector Insights

There are two types of reverses on 1880-CC varieties, both of which can be found inside and outside of GSA holders. The first is the so-called Reverse of '79, where the design centers around an eagle with convex breast feathers of the type normally found on all post-1878 Morgan dollars. The other is the original type of reverse first used in 1878, characterized by its flat breast-feather design. Apparently, a few leftover dies with this "Reverse of '78" found their way into coin presses in 1879 at the San Francisco Mint and in 1880 at the Carson City Mint. The resulting varieties in both cases are intensely collected by variety specialists. Production of 1880-CC silver dollars included two reverse dies with the so-called Reverse of '78, the VAM 4 and the VAM 7, and both are featured in this book. Without question, fortune smiled on GSA collectors, because both Flat Breast varieties are available in the government GSA holders. Indeed, the 1880-CC VAM 4 is in a class by itself, as it is the only Morgan dollar that combines an overdate obverse with a flat-breast reverse from 1878.

Variety Notes

The first of the 1880-CC overdate varieties in terms of VAM number is the VAM 4. It would be difficult to miss this variety when it appears in a GSA case. The partial image of an underlying 7 is readily visible inside the top and bottom loops of the last 8 in the date. And the bottom half of the 0 is filled by the spectacular remains of a 9. The VAM 4 has everything a specialist could possibly want. The eye-catching overdate features are easily visible to the naked eye—no electron microscope needed here! And the so-called Flat Breast reverse die had apparently been left over from coin production not one but *two* years earlier. If you want to be dazzled, just find an example of this variety and study it.

1880-CC
VAM 5

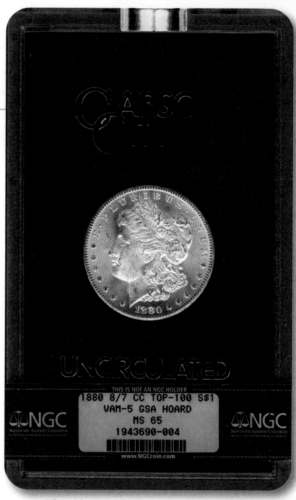

The 1880-CC VAM 5 is the scarcest of the three 80-CC overdates, and its 8/7 overdate feature is plainly visible to the naked eye.

Valuations		GSA	MS-61	MS-62	MS-63	MS-64	MS-65	MS-66
In GSA Case	MS	$625	$650	$800	$1,000	$1,500	$4,000	$17,000
(Graded by NGC)	PL	700	800	900	1,100	2,750	8,000	20,000
	DMPL	800	1,200	2,000	3,500	9,000		
Slabbed	MS		625	650	700	1,100	2,250	5,500
(Not in GSA Case)	PL		675	700	800	1,200	3,000	
	DMPL		700	800	1,500	4,500	19,000	

The so-called High 7 overdate features inside
the second 8 are exciting to collectors.

Note the slanted, non-parallel top arrow
feather that defines the Reverse of '79.

Condition Census

In GSA Case	MS-66
PCGS or NGC	MS-66

1880-CC VAM 5

Collector Insights

The overdate feature inside the second 8 in the date on the 1880-CC VAM 5 is enough to turn the head of even the most jaded variety specialist. Interestingly, not only is an underlying 7 clearly visible behind the 8, but a checkmark can be seen on the top left surface of the last 8. This is important, because a number of 1880-P and 1880-O varieties were found with that checkmark feature; it's been concluded that they are most likely overdates, as well. After all, if the VAM 5 1880-CC has this checkmark *and* definitive overdate markings inside the 8, then other 1880-P, O, and S varieties with only the checkmark were probably overdates, too. Back to VAM 5, a quick glance at the Condition Census data shows that the level of preservation is extremely high for the top specimens, probably because they were spirited away soon after they were minted and remained in the Treasury's possession for almost a century. As they were protected for a hundred years, it stands to reason these cartwheels would be well preserved when they were ultimately distributed to the public in GSA sales.

Variety Notes

Like its VAM 6 counterpart, the 1880-CC VAM 5 obverse is notable for its awe-inspiring 8 Over 7 overdate feature. Both are quite popular with variety specialists. Fortunately, the VAM 5 is available in relatively high grades both inside and outside of GSA holders, although there is a noticeable lack of prooflike and deep mirror prooflike specimens in the highest grading tiers. VAM 5 is known to collectors as the 8 Over 7 High variety, referring to the overdate feature inside the second 8 of the date, which is set high compared to the VAM 6, where it's set lower within the 8. Another distinction is that the bottom of the underlying 7 is flush with the bottom edge of the 8 on VAM 5, whereas the base of the 7 extends below the 8 on the VAM 6. The impressive features of the VAM 5 should be a sure draw to many non-variety collectors down the road, so demand for this variety should vastly increase. The result? Now might be a good time to acquire a high-grade specimen.

1880-CC VAM 6

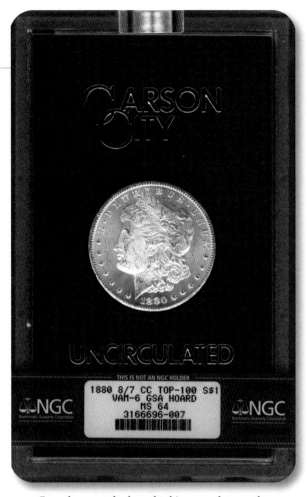

One glance at the breathtaking overdate on the
1880-CC VAM 6 and it's often love at first sight!

Valuations

		GSA	MS-61	MS-62	MS-63	MS-64	MS-65	MS-66
In GSA Case	MS	$575	$700	$900	$1,000	$1,600	$4,750	$18,000
(Graded by NGC)	PL	750	850	950	1,200	2,900	8,500	21,000
	DMPL	950	1,250	2,250	3,750	9,000		
Slabbed	MS							
(Not in GSA Case)	PL							
	DMPL							

Collectors sometimes confuse VAMs 5
and 6, but the key is to note that the
VAM 6 overdate is set lower inside the 8.

Like the 1880-CC VAM 5, the VAM 6 reverse
design displays a slanted arrow feather.

Condition Census

In GSA Case	MS-65
PCGS or NGC	MS-66

1880-CC VAM 6

Collector Insights

In terms of dramatic variety features, many specialists would point to the VAM 6 as *the* overdate in the Morgan dollar series. Basically, the entire underlying 7 is visible inside the two loops of the second 8 in the date. Two faint "ears," which represent the topmost points of the 7, jut up from the top left and top right corners of the 8. The crossbar of the 7 can be seen inside the top loop, while the vertical stem, which stretches down below the 8, is clearly visible inside the bottom loop. The "wow factor" for this variety is off the charts! As if more diagnostics were needed to identify the VAM 6, there is also an area of raised metal along the inside bottom of the 0, which may represent the polishing efforts of the engraver to efface the base of an underlying 9. In any case, obtaining a specimen of the VAM 6 has become a priority for many Morgan dollar collectors, some of whom are not necessarily interested in varieties but recognize a spectacular numismatic item when they see one.

Variety Notes

In terms of 1880-CC overdates, VAM 6 is part of the Big Three, consisting of VAMs 4, 5, and 6. Here, as is the case with the VAM 5, the crossbar of an underlying 7 on the VAM 6 is clearly visible inside the top loop of the second 8 in the date. Also, the vertical shaft of the 7 can be seen inside the lower loop of the 8, and the base of the 7 is discernible below the 8. But to clearly identify a specimen as VAM 6, note that the top of the 7 is lower inside the 8 than on VAM 5. Hence, the VAM 6 is widely known as the "8 Over 7 Low" variety. Another useful diagnostic is the presence of a die scratch through the M of AMERICA on the reverse. The question is this: In American numismatics, how often do you see the almost complete underlying numeral in an overdate variety? Seldom, if ever. Welcome to the world of the 1880-CC VAM 6.

1880-CC
VAM 7
(Reverse of '78)

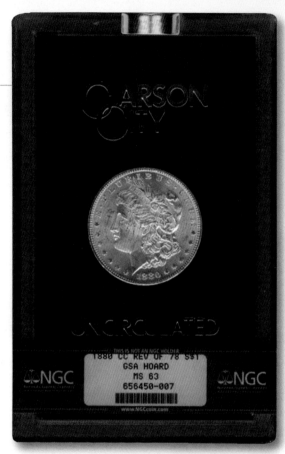

The VAM 7, which is one of only two 1880-CC
varieties with a reverse die from 1878, is
much scarcer than its VAM 4 counterpart.

Valuations

		GSA	MS-61	MS-62	MS-63	MS-64	MS-65	MS-66
In GSA Case	MS	$600	$700	$900	$1,200	$1,700	$6,000	$22,000
(Graded by NGC)	PL	700	825	1,000	1,600	6,000	12,000	
	DMPL	800	900	1,500	5,000	15,000		
Slabbed	MS							
(Not in GSA Case)	PL							
	DMPL							

The 1880-CC VAM 7, which uses a leftover reverse from 1878, is quite an anomaly. This variety and the VAM 4 are the only known examples for which dies from two years earlier have been identified.

The key marker for the VAM 7 obverse, besides its apparent lack of overdate remains inside the 8 of the date, is the "dash" under the second 8.

Condition Census

In GSA Case MS-65
PCGS or NGC..MS-66

Note: The professional grading services to date do not designate VAM 7. The census here is that of the authors' determination.

1880-CC VAM 7 (Reverse of '78)

Collector Insights

Most collectors are aware that pricing guides such as the Greysheet have two listings for 1880-CC. The standard variety has the so-called Round Breast reverse of 1879, which refers to a design where the eagle's breast is raised in relief from the surface level of the coin. Morgan dollar production switched to this design at the Philadelphia Mint in mid-1878, and it continued through 1904. However, a number of reverse dies from early 1878 were apparently left over at the end of 1878 at both western mints. San Francisco used its supply of leftover 1878 Flat Breast dies in 1879, and the Carson City Mint used its in 1880. So, for 1880-CC silver dollars, there are two listed reverse types. (See the illustrations in the 1880-CC VAM 4 listing.) Interestingly, more than 16 different varieties of 1879-S with the 1878 reverse have been cataloged, but there have only been two known varieties of 1880-CC found with this reverse. The first is the VAM 4, featured earlier in this book, and the second is the VAM 7. Take note: though the VAM 4 overdate gets all the glory, it's the VAM 7 that is actually rarer, both inside and outside a GSA case.

Variety Notes

The VAM 7 is considered by many to be a "sleeper" among 1880-CC dollars. It has no overdate features on the obverse, so initially it does little to impress the casual observer. And there are no other exciting obverse design elements to speak of. Then, one might ask, what is there to recommend it? The key is its Reverse of '78, which separates it from all of the Reverse of '79 1880-CC varieties. The VAM 4 is the one other 1880-CC variety with this reverse, but because the VAM 7 is actually the rarer of the two, word has filtered out about its desirability, and there has been a recent explosion of interest in finding this variety in government GSA cases. Not long ago, it was reported that an MS-66 1880-CC VAM 7 sold for $20,000 in a GSA holder. Such figures capture the imagination of countless collectors who have GSA dollars stashed away somewhere in a desk drawer.

1881-CC (GENERIC)

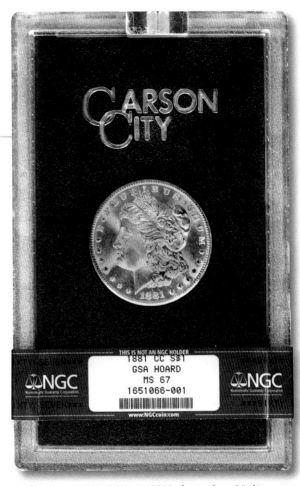

At the Carson City Mint in 1881, fewer than 10 dies were needed to produce the entire original mintage of 296,000.

Valuations		GSA	MS-61	MS-62	MS-63	MS-64	MS-65	MS-66	MS-67
In GSA Case	MS	$600	$600	$650	$690	$825	$1,200	$2,500	$18,000
(Graded by NGC)	PL	600	650	750	1,000	1,500	2,500	4,500	
	DMPL	800	850	1,100	1,750	3,000	7,000	21,000	—
Slabbed	MS		500	550	600	650	1,000	1,500	5,000
(Not in GSA Case)	PL		520	575	625	725	1,500	2,900	
	DMPL		600	650	825	1,400	3,250	8,500	

Carson City silver-dollar production dropped off precipitously in 1881, but the minuscule mintage can be misleading. Today, it is possible to acquire 1881-CC specimens in all grades.

By the Numbers

Original Mintage	296,000
Total GSA Holdings	147,485
Percentage of Mintage in GSA	49.60%
Original Uncirculated Designation	122,709
Not Designated Due to Scratches/Toning etc.	24,776
GSA Overall Rarity Ranking	9th
Non-GSA Rarity Ranking	12th
GSA Prooflike or DMPL Availability	Scarce

Condition Census

In GSA Case	MS-67
PCGS or NGC	MS-68

1881-CC (generic)

Collector Insights

There are two competing factors at work in any discussion of rarity for the 1881-CC silver dollar. On the one hand, an original mintage of only 296,000 should, under normal circumstances, translate into its being an ultra-rare Morgan dollar. After all, this official mintage is the fifth-lowest in the entire Morgan dollar series! But there is something else at work. It turns out that a huge percentage of the original mintage was found to have survived in the GSA holdings. Specifically, 147,485 specimens (or nearly half of the entire original mintage) survived in government vaults, and now all of these coins are in the hands of collectors. The bottom line is that, today, 1881-CC as a date is not a major rarity. Furthermore, it should not surprise anyone that large numbers of extremely high-grade specimens exist. After all, these silver dollars were kept in a protected environment for almost a century. Even so, NGC has slabbed 4 specimens in MS-68, 161 in MS-67, and some 1,200+ in MS-66; that's a lot of coins in remarkably high grades. And, in GSA holders, 23 in MS-67 and 325 in MS-66 is an enormous number of top-end coins for the market to absorb. When all is said and done, it's easy to see why the 1881-CC, even with its high survival rate in high quality, is a "must-have" date for the quality-conscious collector.

Variety Notes

When is an overdate not an overdate? It's not a trick question. The 1881-CC VAM 2 displays what many experts in the past believed was an overdate feature in the second 8 of the date. Look closely and you'll see what appears to be the crossbar of an underlying 7. No less a numismatic scholar than Walter Breen was convinced that these markings represented an overdate, and here's what he said about it in his *Complete Encyclopedia of U.S. and Colonial Coins*: "Earliest state of VAM 2; crossbar of 7 within upper loop of second 8. Independently discovered by this writer and Art Morano." However, most specialists today disagree with Breen. Leroy Van Allen, for instance, has indicated that he believes the so-called overdate is actually nothing more than a "band of die chips" that "look like" an overdate feature. How's that for letting all the air out of the balloon! In any case, for many collectors and researchers, this interplay makes coin collecting that much more interesting.

1881-CC
VAM 2

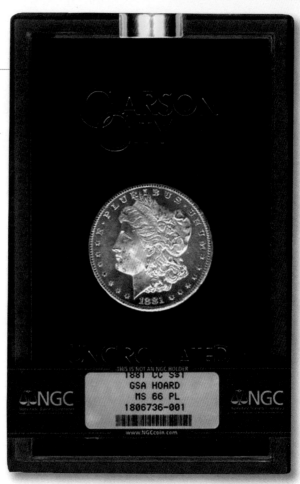

The 1881-CC varieties generate little excitement for most collectors, except for the VAM 2, with markings inside the second 8 of the date that mimic an overdate.

Valuations

		GSA	MS-61	MS-62	MS-63	MS-64	MS-65	MS-66	MS-67
In GSA Case	MS	$600	$600	$650	$700	$900	$2,000	$2,800	$20,000
(Graded by NGC)	PL	700	750	825	1,050	1,500	3,000	5,750	—
	DMPL	850	900	1,200	2,000	3,000	7,000	21,000	
Slabbed	MS								
(Not in GSA Case)	PL								
	DMPL								

There are a number of features to attribute the 1881-CC VAM 2,
including a die scratch above the top arrow feather on the reverse,
but the unique second 8 in the date remains the key diagnostic.

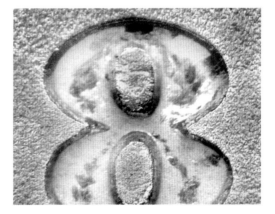

The distinctive markings in the top loop of the
8 may be a die gouge, die chips, or the remains
of an underlying 7. Even the experts can't decide!

Condition Census

In GSA Case	MS-66
PCGS or NGC	MS-66

Note: The professional grading services to date do not designate VAM 2. The census here is that of the
authors' determination.

1881-CC VAM 2

Collector Insights

As a date, 1881-CC is not noted for its die varieties, and only six die pairs have been cataloged by Van Allen and Mallis. These include four or five different obverses and a similar number of reverse dies. While there are no standout varieties in terms of rarity, the VAM 2 has generated some excitement. The controversial markings in the top loop of the second 8 in the date are viewed by some as the remaining artifacts of an underlying 7. Also, the proximity of 1881 to the series of spectacular overdates of the preceding year has added fuel to the fire. The discussion rages on, but up to this point there has been little or no added premium for the VAM 2 over the generic 1881-CC. And even in a GSA case, the variety premium has been small.

One observation: It's clear from the Condition Census chart on the previous page that few, if any, VAM 2 specimens have reflective surfaces, and it's interesting that NGC hasn't graded any of this variety above MS-65. Who's to say, but it's possible that a top-end VAM 2 with DMPL surfaces might fetch a surprising price in tomorrow's marketplace.

Variety Notes

If you like a bit of controversy to stir up the pot, the 1881-CC VAM 2 is for you. Is it an overdate or not? People have lined up on both sides of the issue, but it is a testimony to Van Allen's influence that the tide of opinion has shifted to the idea that the metal inside the second 8 of the date is merely the product of some die chips. In any case, the VAM 2 has some other interesting variety features, including the fact that both 8's are doubled. The first 8 shows doubling at the top inside of the lower loop, and the second 8 is doubled on the right inside of the lower loop. The VAM 2 also shows a doubled-die reverse, where UNITED STATES of AMERICA and the motto "In God We Trust" both display doubling. The bottom line is that the 1881-CC should continue to be the subject of lively discussion in the numismatic community for some time to come—find a specimen and weigh in on the debate!

1882-CC
(GENERIC)

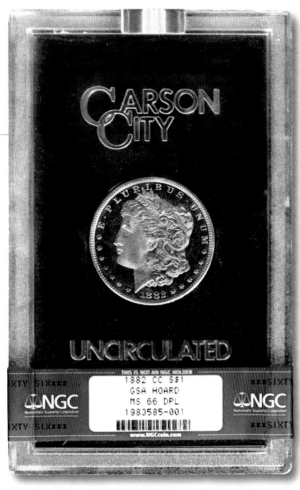

More than 600,000 1882-CC-dated silver dollars
were distributed to the public through GSA sales.

Valuations

		GSA	MS-61	MS-62	MS-63	MS-64	MS-65	MS-66	MS-67
In GSA Case	MS	$225	$250	$275	$300	$325	$700	$2,500	$22,500
(Graded by NGC)	PL	250	275	325	425	475	1,150	4,500	
	DMPL	300	350	450	800	1,100	4,900	22,500	
Slabbed	MS		225	250	275	300	650	1,250	
(Not in GSA Case)	PL		250	275	300	325	700	2,350	12,500
	DMPL		285	325	550	750	2,000	4,250	35,000

Collector interest in the 1882-CC VAM 2 has greatly
increased, due in part to its inclusion in the variety book,
Official Guide to the Hit List 40.

By the Numbers

Original Mintage	1,133,000
Total GSA Holdings	605,029
Percentage of Mintage in GSA	44.60%
Original Uncirculated Designation	382,913
Not Designated Due to Scratches/Toning etc.	222,116
GSA Overall Rarity Ranking	11th
Non-GSA Rarity Ranking	10th
GSA Prooflike or DMPL Availability	More than 100

Condition Census

In GSA Case	MS-67
PCGS or NGC	MS-67

1882-CC (generic)

Collector Insights

The year 1882 is notable as the first of three years in which Morgan dollar production was near its peak at the Carson City Mint. A little over 1.1 million silver dollars were struck that year, but with only limited demand for these cartwheels in most of the West, a large portion of that output ended up back in the U.S. Treasury vaults. And so, the 1882-CC, along with the 1883-CC and 1884-CC, is considered a common Carson City coin today.

Confirmation of that fact can be found in the Greysheet listed prices, which currently begin in low-grade Very Good at $75, but in MS-63 increase up to only $260. The same is true of this date in GSA holders, where the 1882-CC is readily available in all grades up to MS-66. Indeed, dealers who specialize in GSA dollars often have stacks of the 1882-CC at coin shows to sell to the public. That said, the greatest opportunity for collectors may rest in the seldom-encountered prooflike and deep mirror prooflike specimens of this date.

Variety Notes

Not only are few GSA dollar specialists aware of the six known varieties of the 1882-CC, but VAM collectors are mostly in the dark, as well. Why? Only one stands out from the rest, the VAM 2, which is featured in this book. The 1882-CC VAM 2 represents, at least in our minds, one of the important future directions numismatics is taking. In the mid-1880s, generally only a coin's date was important to collectors. Late in the century, the mintmark became an essential element of coin collecting. Then, in the mid-1900s, the popularity of die varieties seemed to explode, generating renewed interest in many U.S. coin series. True, early copper coinage had been collected by variety for decades, but modern coins like Lincoln cents and Morgan dollars weren't. What's next? Die states. We're already seeing it happen with some ultra-late-die-state silver dollar varieties bringing huge premiums. So, the 1882-CC VAM 2, with its four discernible die states, may be a harbinger of the future!

1882-CC VAM 2

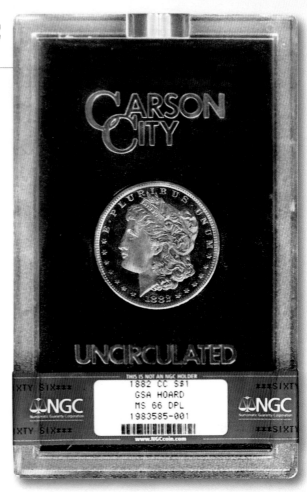

Current research indicates that there are four
critical die states for the 1882-CC VAM 2, and
each one is becoming its own collectible variety.

Valuations		GSA	MS-61	MS-62	MS-63	MS-64	MS-65	MS-66	MS-67
In GSA Case	MS	$250	$275	$300	$350	$650	$825	$3,000	$25,000
(Graded by NGC)	PL	300	325	450	675	850	1,300	5,500	
	DMPL	400	500	650	900	1,200	6,000		
Slabbed	MS								
(Not in GSA Case)	PL								
	DMPL								

First and foremost, the 1882-CC VAM 2 can easily
be identified by the raised "dot" of metal on the
surface of the upper left loop of the second 8.

On early die states there is a curved line under
the first 8, which is thought to represent the top
of an underlying "1" that's been polished away.

Condition Census

In GSA Case	MS-65
PCGS or NGC	MS-66

Note: The professional grading services to date do not designate VAM 2. The census here is that of the
authors' determination.

1882-CC VAM 2

Collector Insights

For those GSA specialists who want to branch out into some of the die varieties found in GSA holders, the 1882-CC VAM 2 represents fertile ground for exploration. It's the only Carson City dollar that has four different die states listed in the current VAM book supplements. And Van Allen has assigned an R-4 rarity rating to the first die state, R-5 to the middle two, and R-6 to the late die state, so the inference is that these varieties become scarcer (and more desirable) as one moves later in the die states. Now might be the time to acquire a specimen of the ultra-late-stage VAM 2C variety, which displays several awe-inspiring die breaks on the obverse. Apparently, severe clashing weakened the die, and as a result metal from the obverse die broke away in at least two locations. This may be the best example of a "counter-clash" in the Morgan dollar series. Clashed dies are common, but multiple clashings, where the clashed image is transferred back to the original die, is an extremely rare phenomenon. So check your 1882-CC dollars for the various stages and effects.

Variety Notes

The 1882-CC VAM 2 is a two-sided marvel, with its repunched date on the obverse and its doubled UNITED STATES OF AMERICA on the reverse. The first 8 is doubled along the top, the second 8 is strongly doubled on the left side, and the 2 is doubled at the top outside. But more importantly, four die states are known for this variety. The early die state shows what appears to be the top of an extra 1 below the first 8. The second die state, which is now the VAM 2A, is clashed with a faint "n" in front of Liberty's neck. The VAM 2B is a polished-down version of the VAM 2A. And, finally, the *pièce de résistance*: VAM 2C, which no longer shows the misplaced 1, is the fascinating ultra-late die state with large breaks on Liberty's lip and behind her cap, caused by multiple clashing. These die stages are so important that the 1882-CC VAM 2 has been included in the official Hit List 40 listings, which represent the most significant Morgan dollar varieties not already included in the Top 100 and Hot 50 books.

1883-CC
(GENERIC)

With more than 750,000 specimens in the
GSA hoard, the generic 1883-CC is readily
obtainable in all grades through MS-66.

Valuations		GSA	MS-61	MS-62	MS-63	MS-64	MS-65	MS-66	MS-67
In GSA Case	MS	$200	$225	$250	$275	$300	$625	$1,250	$16,500
(Graded by NGC)	PL	225	250	300	400	450	800	2,650	—
	DMPL	250	300	500	700	850	4,000	15,000	—
Slabbed	MS		225	250	270	350	575	1,000	4,500
(Not in GSA Case)	PL		275	300	350	450	700	1,250	9,000
	DMPL		300	325	425	650	1,500	3,000	27,500

The 1883-CC, even with substantial representation in the
GSA holdings, is not widely thought of in terms of varieties.

By the Numbers

Original Mintage	1,204,000
Total GSA Holdings	755,518
Percentage of Mintage in GSA	62.70%
Original Uncirculated Designation	523,853
Not Designated Due to Scratches/Toning etc.	231,665
GSA Overall Rarity Ranking	12th
Non-GSA Rarity Ranking	13th
GSA Prooflike or DMPL Availability	More than 100

Condition Census

In GSA Case	MS-67
PCGS or NGC	MS-68

1883-CC (generic)

Collector Insights

It was a great idea whose time had come—building a U.S. branch mint near the source of the most fabulous silver strike in history. It made sense to construct a mint at Carson City, Nevada, in close proximity to the Comstock Lode mines, but there were significant challenges, as well. Raw materials were exceedingly expensive to procure, personnel were difficult to attract, and the actual cost of striking coins in Carson City, compared with the other U.S. mints, really tells the story. In the mid-1880s, coining costs at the Carson City Mint were more than four times the per-unit costs at the Philadelphia and New Orleans mints, and almost double those of its western counterpart, the San Francisco Mint. The end result was that it was just too expensive to strike silver dollars at Carson City, especially considering the minimal demand for these coins. Of 1.2 million silver dollars struck in 1883 at the Carson City Mint, more than 60 percent ended up in bags stored in U.S. Treasury vaults. Once all the government holdings were encased and distributed to collectors, it's no wonder the 1883-CC Morgan dollar became one of the most readily available CC dollars.

Variety Notes

Even with its original mintage of more than a million, the 1883-CC has had only a limited number of die pairs identified and cataloged by Van Allen and Mallis. Up to this point, 13 different varieties have been attributed, consisting of eight different die pairs and five significant die-clashed subvarieties. It's interesting that most of the variations for the 1883-CC occur on the obverse, since there are only five different reverse dies known for the entire production of silver dollars that year. VAMs 3 and 6 are Dash varieties, with a horizontal line under the second 8 of the date; and VAMs 4, 5, 6, 7, and 8 are Repunched Date varieties. VAM 4 is most important in terms of collector interest.

1883-CC
VAM 4

Although the 1883-CC VAM 4 is not on the radar screens of many collectors, its strongly doubled date is exciting enough to ultimately become a major attraction.

Valuations		GSA	MS-61	MS-62	MS-63	MS-64	MS-65	MS-66	MS-67
In GSA Case	MS	$225	$250	$275	$350	$525	$700	$1,500	$18,000
(Graded by NGC)	PL	250	300	400	500	750	850	2,700	—
	DMPL	300	425	600	750	950	4,000	13,500	—
Slabbed	MS								
(Not in GSA Case)	PL								
	DMPL								

The incomplete remains of several underlying
digits can be observed inside and around
the individual numerals of the date.

Condition Census

In GSA Case	MS-66
PCGS or NGC	MS-66

Note: The professional grading services to date do not designate VAM 4. The census here is that of the authors' determination.

1883-CC VAM 4

Collector Insights

It's not that the original mintage of the 1883-CC was particularly large. In fact, at 1.2 million, the 1883-CC is in the bottom quarter of all Morgan dollar mintages. But as a date, the 1883-CC is common today (if any Carson City date can be called "common"), because 60 percent of the original mintage survived in government vaults as part of the GSA hoard. Much of it endured in pristine condition, since the bags of Carson City silver dollars remained unopened during the intervening century. A quick glance at the Condition Census for this date shows that the entire chart consists of coins in MS-67 condition, so quality is not a problem! Even better, early-die-state prooflike and deep mirror prooflike specimens are often available, further adding to the collectability of this date. As might be expected, the GSA encountered some difficulty in selling all the 1883-CC and 1884-CC dates as part of the GSA sales; there were just too many for the market to readily absorb. But all that is history today, as collectors fixate on any silver dollar with the historic CC mintmark.

Variety Notes

The VAM 4 Doubled Date variety has everything a collector could want in terms of variety features. The date area, where all the action is, shows the stunning effects of a date-positioning error, in which the original date was incorrectly set into the die at an angle. The result? The left end of the date was set too low and the right end too high. When the date was then repositioned correctly, it left some intriguing remains on the die; namely, the 1 is doubled on the right side, the first 8 shows doubling inside the top loop, the second 8 is doubled at the top outside, and a patch of metal is visible high over the 3. Add to this the presence of a dash under the second 8, which served as the fulcrum for the tilted date, and you have the framework for some wild doubling. Repunched dates are common in the Morgan dollar series, but not like this one!

1884-CC (Generic)

Total production at all four U.S. Mints in 1884 amounted to more than 27 million silver dollars. Of these, only slightly over one million were struck at the Carson City Mint. Why so few? Mint officials calculated that the per-unit cost of each silver dollar produced at Carson City was higher than at any of the other mints.

Valuations		GSA	MS-61	MS-62	MS-63	MS-64	MS-65	MS-66	MS-67
In GSA Case	MS	$200	$225	$250	$275	$300	$625	$1,250	$16,500
(Graded by NGC)	PL	225	250	300	400	450	800	2,650	—
	DMPL	250	300	500	700	850	4,000	15,000	—
Slabbed	MS		225	250	270	350	575	1,000	4,500
(Not in GSA Case)	PL		275	300	350	450	700	1,500	7,500
	DMPL		300	325	425	650	1,500	3,500	27,500

The 1884-CC is hardly a date known for its varieties, even though the original mintage was quite large by Carson City Mint standards.

By the Numbers

Original Mintage	1,136,000
Total GSA Holdings	962,638
Percentage of Mintage in GSA	84.60%
Original Uncirculated Designation	788,630
Not Designated Due to Scratches/Toning etc.	174,008
GSA Overall Rarity Ranking	13th
Non-GSA Rarity Ranking	11th
GSA Prooflike or DMPL Availability	More than 100

Condition Census

In GSA Case	MS-67
PCGS or NGC	MS-68

1884-CC (generic)

Collector Insights

It was reported that, of the 2,937,695 silver dollars contained in the GSA holdings, more than 960,000 consisted of a single date, 1884-CC. That gives the 1884-CC the distinction of being the most heavily hoarded silver dollar in American history. And given its original mintage of 1.1 million, more than 85 percent was ultimately distributed to collectors. This doesn't sound like the prescription for a rare date—and it's not. The 1884-CC, either in a GSA hard case, slabbed, or raw, is readily available, although it's true that *all* CC dollars are worth a significant premium due to the Carson City mystique. In 1884, coinage costs were excessively high at the Carson City Mint, and they rose to a breaking point in 1885. So it's not surprising that 1.2 million silver dollars were produced in 1883, 1.1 million in 1884, and only 228,000 in 1885. The upshot is that the typical 1884-CC may be at the bottom of the food chain when it comes to Carson City dollars.

Variety Notes

The 1884-CC is a variety collector's dream come true. Rather than the usual number of five or six varieties, like so many of the CC dates, there are about a dozen different cataloged 1884-CC varieties, and many are quite interesting. For instance, VAMs 3, 7, and 11 all show spectacular doubling in the date, and it's *not* the kind that requires a high-powered microscope to see. These varieties show extra metal around and inside the numerals of the date, to the point that many viewers probably have never seen such bungled numbers on a U.S. silver dollar. VAM 4 is a Spiked Date with doubling on the 1 and lines on the surfaces of the numbers. And as the VAM 4 obverse die continued in use, extraneous gouges and die breaks came into play. Check your 1884-CC GSA cases for an exciting array of varieties.

1884-CC
VAM 2

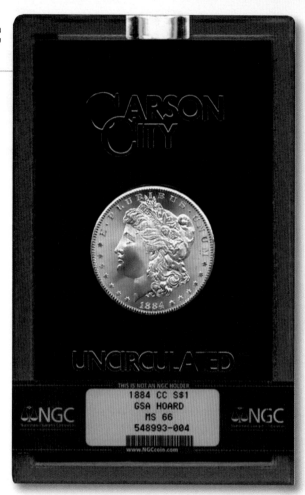

In terms of dramatic effects, the doubling on the first two digits of the date on this 1884-CC VAM 2 is among the most notable in the Morgan dollar series.

Valuations

		GSA	MS-61	MS-62	MS-63	MS-64	MS-65	MS-66	MS-67
In GSA Case	MS	$200	$250	$300	$350	$525	$750	$1,500	$18,500
(Graded by NGC)	PL	250	300	370	500	750	900	2,800	—
	DMPL		400	475	750	1,000	5,000	16,500	
Slabbed	MS								
(Not in GSA Case)	PL								
	DMPL								

Artifacts from an underlying date are clearly
visible on the 1884-CC VAM 2 variety.

Here is a close-up of the 1 in the date, where
extra metal at the top offers a clue that the
original date was set too high and then corrected.

Condition Census

In GSA Case	MS-65
PCGS or NGC	MS-67

Note: The professional grading services to date do not designate VAM 2. The census here is that of the
authors' determination.

1884-CC VAM 2

Collector Insights

The 1884-CC is the poster child for 19th-century silver dollars that failed to circulate and ended up back in government vaults. There, some 962,637 specimens of the 1884-CC quietly rested for almost a hundred years, to be distributed during the 1970s in four of the seven GSA sales. The first sale, in late 1972, put 267,733 coins of this date into the hands of collectors, dealers, and investors. The next sale, in mid-1973, released another 64,384 specimens of the 1884-CC. This was followed by a mid-1974 sale that contained another 28,349 coins. Finally, after a gap of six years, the last of the 1884-CC coins were sold in February 1980. The point to keep in mind is that it took four GSA sales to distribute the colossal quantity of this date, which amounted to almost a million specimens. But for variety specialists, this kind of mintage invariably leads to numerous interesting types. Sure enough, some fascinating varieties are found on 1884-dated CC dollars. In particular, repunched dates abound, as well as other interesting variety features. Borrow a VAM book and look at VAMs 2, 3, 4, and 11.

Variety Notes

In many ways, Carson City silver dollars represent one of the last frontiers of silver-dollar variety collecting. Why? On the one hand, legions of collectors specialize only in GSA dollars, while on the other, there are large numbers of hobbyists who collect VAMs. Only rarely do silver-dollar collectors focus on both. The concept of this book is to produce a synergy that combines both areas of interest. Take the VAM 2 as an example. This variety displays strong doubling along the tops of the 18 of the date, lots of extra metal, and a dramatic die break that connects both numerals. If this same effect were found on, say, an 1878 silver dollar, it would warrant a press release and lots of publicity! But such varieties languish among Carson City dollars, and therein lies the opportunity.

1885-CC
(GENERIC)

The 1885-CC Morgan dollar had the fourth-lowest
mintage of any Morgan dollar. Only the 1895-P, 1893-S,
and 1894-P dollars were produced in lesser quantities.

Valuations

		GSA	MS-61	MS-62	MS-63	MS-64	MS-65	MS-66	MS-67
In GSA Case	MS	$700	$750	$775	$1,000	$1,250	$2,000	$4,500	$35,000
(Graded by NGC)	PL	750	850	925	1,150	2,000	3,250	10,500	
	DMPL	800	925	1,200	2,000	3,700	8,500	—	
Slabbed	MS		775	800	850	850	1,300	2,350	12,000
(Not in GSA Case)	PL		800	825	850	950	2,500	3,200	14,000
	DMPL		900	950	1,100	1,500	3,000	11,500	55,000

Current thinking is that it may have taken only three obverse and two reverse dies to produce the entire original mintage of 228,000 1885-CC coins.

By the Numbers

Original Mintage	228,000
Total GSA Holdings	148,285
Percentage of Mintage in GSA	64.90%
Original Uncirculated Designation	130,823
Not Designated Due to Scratches/Toning etc.	17,462
GSA Overall Rarity Ranking	10th
Non-GSA Rarity Ranking	9th
GSA Prooflike or DMPL Availability	Scarce

Condition Census

In GSA Case	MS-67
PCGS or NGC	MS-68

1885-CC (generic)

Collector Insights

One event in particular affected the shaky political situation at the Carson City Mint in 1885. On March 8, its well-respected superintendent, James Crawford, passed away, and with his death Washington's political support quickly evaporated. There had already been signs of trouble, but within three weeks of Crawford's passing, all coinage production at the Mint was suspended. In a final statement of no confidence, the Carson City Mint was officially closed on November 6, 1885. This partial-year shutdown helps to explain the miniscule CC production of only 228,000 silver dollars in 1885, the fourth-lowest mintage of any Morgan dollar from 1878 to 1921. But what's amazing is that so little of this mintage actually entered circulation. The GSA hoard contained slightly more than 148,000 of those 1885-CC dollars, which represents about 65 percent of the entire original mintage! Even so, the 1885-CC remains popular with collectors, including those who specialize in GSA dollars. After a four-year interruption, the coining presses at the Carson City Mint were again cranked up in 1889, but total production never reached the peak level of the early years.

Variety Notes

1885-CC, as a date, has a strikingly small list of known die varieties. Why? The entire original mintage of just 228,000 was probably struck with only three or four sets of dies. Of the four known die pairs, there are two Dash varieties, one variety with no significant variety features, and another with the CC mintmark tilted to the left. But, fortunately for VAM collectors, one of the Dash varieties is a megastar that has captured the imaginations (and pocketbooks!) of collectors as part of the HOT 50 listings. That variety, the VAM 4, is showcased in this book. In terms of popularity, the fact that the 1885-CC has the lowest original mintage of any CC dollar certainly doesn't hurt its overall appeal in a market where Carson City dollars are a hot commodity.

1885-CC
VAM 4

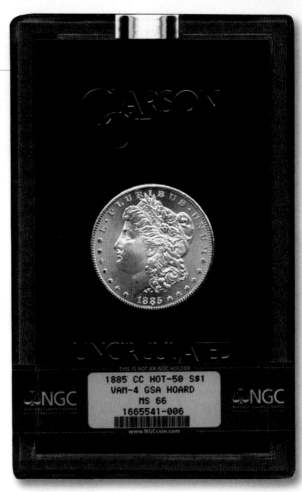

While many Morgan dollars show faint "engraver's dashes" under the second 8 in the date, the 1885-CC VAM 4 is extraordinary for the actual size of the dash.

Valuations

		GSA	MS-61	MS-62	MS-63	MS-64	MS-65	MS-66	MS-67
In GSA Case	MS	$800	$850	$925	$1,000	$1,400	$2,500	$6,000	$50,000
(Graded by NGC)	PL								
	DMPL								
Slabbed	MS								
(Not in GSA Case)	PL								
	DMPL								

Note the "Super Dash" under the second 8 in the date—
the largest such dash on any Morgan dollar obverse.

Condition Census

In GSA Case	MS-65
PCGS or NGC	MS-66

1885-CC VAM 4

Collector Insights

The 1885-CC VAM 4 is a new option for many GSA specialists, although it is well established in VAM collecting circles. The upshot is that the VAM 4 "Super Dash" variety is only now commanding a significant premium when found in a GSA holder. It's safe to say that any variety enthusiast would be impressed with the die-break feature on the VAM 4 under the second 8 in the date. Actually, the obverse die was weakened in the area just below the 8 when a dash mark was punched into the die to correctly position the date over it. This was normal for this era of silver-dollar production, but here a piece of the die face broke out. The effect is startling. Close examination shows that the die actually broke in two stages, with what mimics doubling along the bottom edge of the break. Collectors often note that the ultimate effect is similar to the 1880-CC overdates, where the base of the underlying 7 protrudes out from under the 8. So the assumption is that VAM 4 must be an overdate variety. However, this is not the case. The truth is even more interesting, as broken dies involving the date area on Morgan dollars are quite rare and typically bring very significant premiums.

Variety Notes

The 1885-CC VAM 4 represents a unique type of variety. In order to position the date onto the die in the precisely correct location, Mint engravers marked the 10th denticle to the right of Liberty's neck with a dash mark. The third digit of the date was then centered over this dash, at which time the entire date could be punched into the die. The final step was to remove this orientation mark from the die — at least, that was the theory. Most of the time the dash was successfully removed, but in a number of instances all or part of it was inadvertently left on the die. Even worse, in the case of the 1885-CC VAM 4, the area between the dash and the bottom of the numeral above it was weakened to the point that a piece actually broke out of the die. To the delight of variety specialists, the resulting dash on the VAM 4 is the largest found on any Morgan dollar obverse.

1889-CC
(GENERIC)

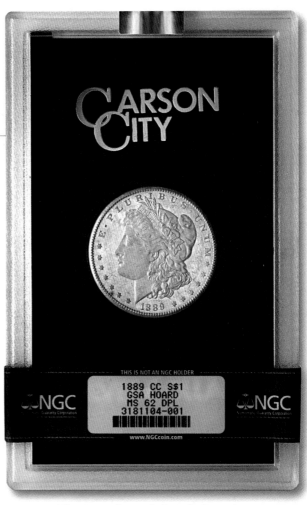

After years of speculation, the legendary
1889-CC coin featured here recently came to
light. It remains one of a kind in a GSA case.

Valuations		GSA	MS-61	MS-62	MS-63	MS-64	MS-65
In GSA Case	MS						
(Graded by NGC)	PL						
	DMPL			—			
Slabbed	MS		$30,000	$37,500	$47,500	$90,000	$325,000
(Not in GSA Case)	PL		32,500	37,500	50,000	95,000	375,000
	DMPL		35,000	40,000	57,500	100,000	

Already popular as a date due to its extreme
rarity, the 1889-CC is considered one of the
top five key dates in the Morgan dollar series.

By the Numbers

Original Mintage	350,000
Total GSA Holdings	1
Percentage of Mintage in GSA	
Original Uncirculated Designation	0
Not Designated Due to Scratches/Toning etc.	1
GSA Overall Rarity Ranking	Tied 1st
Non-GSA Rarity Ranking	1st
GSA Prooflike or DMPL Availability	Unique

Condition Census

In GSA Case	Unique MS-62PL
PCGS or NGC	MS-64PL

1889-CC (generic)

Collector Insights

In 1889, U.S. silver dollars once again were struck at the Carson City Mint after a four-year hiatus. But it was hardly a boom time for silver-dollar production, as a mere 350,000 cartwheels were coined. Of course, the surviving mintages are considerably less than that. Simply put, the 1889-CC silver dollar is one of the rarest, most sought-after dates in the entire Morgan dollar series. This brings us to the question, how many 1889-CC dollars ended up in GSA cases? If the reported numbers are correct, the answer is a grand total of . . . *one*. That's right, only a single 1889-CC was listed as part of the government hoard, and amid much excitement, that specimen finally surfaced in the summer of 2008. Once this legendary prize was corroborated, it was submitted to NGC for grading, and much to the delight of its owners, came back MS-62DMPL! And the price? The high-six-figure, low-seven-figure range has been bandied about, but it may turn out to be a bargain at any price, if one hopes to complete a GSA dollar set.

Variety Notes

When it comes to the 1889-CC, collectors basically can forget about die varieties. None is presently more significant than the rest, and regarding the one specimen that's now entered the spotlight, no one's likely to ask what variety it is. Indeed, acquiring an 1889-CC in a GSA holder is such a landmark event that it warrants trumpet fanfare and a week-long celebration. If there exists a variety fanatic to whom 1889-CC die varieties *are* important, then consider that there are only three die pairs cataloged by Van Allen and Mallis for the entire 1889-CC mintage. Of these, one obverse die shows a repunched 1 in the date, and another has the date punched out of position, slightly to the right of normal. That's about it. So forget about the variety—just find another specimen or acquire this one!

1890-CC
(GENERIC)

The 1890-CC, although not an ultra-rarity outside a GSA case, is one of the scarcest Carson City dollars in a GSA holder.

Valuations

		GSA	MS-61	MS-62	MS-63	MS-64	MS-65	MS-66	MS-67
In GSA Case	MS	$4,000	$4,500	$5,000	$7,500	$18,000	—		
(Graded by NGC)	PL								
	DMPL								
Slabbed	MS		500	600	900	1,800	$5,750	$25,000	$40,000
(Not in GSA Case)	PL		525	625	1,000	2,200	9,800	26,000	
	DMPL		600	750	1,500	3,500	14,000		

It has been estimated that as little as one-tenth of one percent of
the original 1890-CC mintage found its way into the GSA holdings.

By the Numbers

Original Mintage	2,309,041
Total GSA Holdings	3,949
Percentage of Mintage in GSA	0.10%
Original Uncirculated Designation	3,610
Not Designated Due to Scratches/Toning etc.	339
GSA Overall Rarity Ranking	4th
Non-GSA Rarity Ranking	6th
GSA Prooflike or DMPL Availability	Excessively Rare

Condition Census

In GSA Case	MS-64
PCGS or NGC	MS-65

1890-CC (generic)

Collector Insights

From a historical perspective, U.S. silver-dollar production has always been more of a political issue than a question of demand. At no time was this truer than the last quarter of the 19th century, when there was a pitched battle raging in the halls of Congress over the role of silver in our coinage. The resulting mintages of silver dollars fluctuated wildly, from more than 21.7 million at the Philadelphia Mint in 1889, all the way down to 100,000 four years later at the San Francisco Mint. One key factor in the discussions was the decline in the price of silver bullion. By 1890 silver had fallen below 90 cents per troy ounce, and since the Treasury was mandated by law to produce silver dollars based on acquiring a set dollar-amount of silver, increased production was required. The result? In 1890 more than 38 million silver dollars had to be minted, and that virtual explosion of coins even carried over to the Carson City Mint, where 2.3 million cartwheels were struck. That figure represents the highest silver-dollar production for any year at this Western mint. Still, the 1890-CC has turned out to be a scarce coin, particularly inside a GSA holder. This may be the consequence of melting large quantities of silver dollars as part of the Pittman Act of 1918, but whatever the case, few specimens remained as part of the government hoard. Now, collectors are surprised to learn that, other than the three virtually unobtainable dates, 1890-CC is actually the rarest of all the CC dollars in a GSA holder.

Variety Notes

Whereas many Carson City dates have such small mintages that only a few dies were required to produce the entire mintage, the total number of silver dollars struck in 1890 exceeded 2 million. As a result, more than a dozen die varieties are known for the 1890-CC. These varieties include repunched dates, doubled mintmarks, and date-placement varieties. But only one has grabbed the attention of variety specialists, the whimsically named "Tailbar" variety. Assigned as VAM 4 by Van Allen and Mallis, the Tailbar variety in Mint State condition is one of the highlights of the highly vaunted TOP 100 listings. As for the 1890-CC date, it might be worth noting that 8 of the top 10 slabbed (non-GSA) specimens are either prooflike or deep mirror prooflike examples, yet none of the top 10 specimens in a GSA case is either prooflike or deep mirror prooflike. Do you hear an opportunity knocking?

1890-CC VAM 4

Looking for a spectacular variety in a GSA
case? The 1890-CC VAM 4 would be the
one to find, since the wildly popular "Tailbar"
variety is on every VAM collector's hit list. But up
to this point none has been found in a GSA case.

Valuations		GSA	MS-61	MS-62	MS-63	MS-64	MS-65	MS-66
In GSA Case	MS							
(Graded by NGC)	PL							
	DMPL							
Slabbed	MS		$2,000	$3,000	$5,000	$6,500	$37,500	
(Not in GSA Case)	PL							
	DMPL							

Few variety features in the Morgan dollar series can match
the prominence of the "Tailbar" on the 1890-CC VAM 4.

Condition Census

In GSA Case	Choice Uncirculated
PCGS or NGC	MS-63

Note: The professional grading services to date do not designate VAM 4. The census here is that of the
authors' determination.

Collector Insights

Outside of a GSA case, the 1890-CC Tailbar variety is one of the best-of-the-best TOP 100 VAMs, bringing huge premiums in high-end brilliant Uncirculated grades. But no Tailbar VAM 4 specimens have yet been found in either a GSA hard plastic case or in a GSA Blue Pack, and that's the reason the VAM 4 is included here. Even though the wildly popular Tailbar variety hasn't turned up in a GSA holder, no one is prepared to say none exists. After all, when VAM collecting was in its infancy, very few uncirculated Tailbar varieties were known. But that all changed when an army of VAM specialists starting combing the marketplace and the inventories of collectors. The same may hold true of Tailbar specimens in GSA holders; they may exist, but more eyes are required to find them. In any case, the reward for locating a VAM 4 Tailbar variety, either in a GSA hard case or in a soft pack, would warrant a trek by Indiana Jones to the middle of the Amazon jungle.

Variety Notes

The highly coveted Tailbar variety is easy to identify, so it's not because of attribution difficulties that GSA specimens remain unknown. To the contrary, the VAM 4 displays one of the most dramatic die gouges in the entire Morgan dollar series, and collectors have been in pursuit of this variety for decades. Part of its appeal derives from the fact that its breathtaking variety feature can be seen with the naked eye. A raised line of metal runs from the junction of the eagle's leftmost tail feathers and the arrow feathers down to the left wreath. In fact, the feature is so obvious that it might be mistaken for part of the principal design. There's no other Morgan dollar variety quite like it! The dilemma for GSA collectors is that this celebrated variety is not known in a GSA holder. Ready for your name up in lights? Find one of these in a GSA case.

1891-CC
(GENERIC)

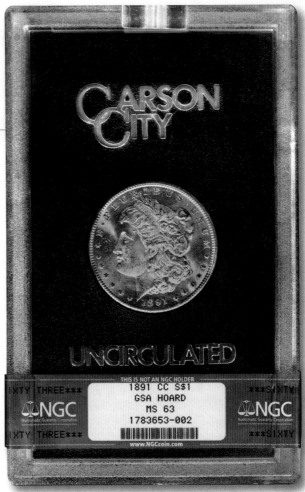

Like its 1890-CC counterpart, the 1891-CC is much rarer in a GSA holder than it is outside one of the government cases.

Valuations		GSA	MS-61	MS-62	MS-63	MS-64	MS-65	MS-66	MS-67
In GSA Case	MS	$3,000	$3,250	$4,000	$5,500	$25,000			
(Graded by NGC)	PL								
	DMPL								
Slabbed	MS		450	510	900	1,500	$5,000	$15,000	$37,500
(Not in GSA Case)	PL		500	650	1,000	1,600	7,500	15,000	
	DMPL		625	1,250	1,800	4,500	32,500		

A total of only 5,687 specimens of the 1891-CC ultimately found
their way into the hands of collectors, as part of the GSA hoard.

By the Numbers

Original Mintage	1,618,000
Total GSA Holdings	5,687
Percentage of Mintage in GSA	0.30%
Original Uncirculated Designation	5,177
Not Designated Due to Scratches/Toning etc.	510
GSA Overall Rarity Ranking	6th
Non-GSA Rarity Ranking	4th
GSA Prooflike or DMPL Availability	Excessively Rare

Condition Census

In GSA Case	MS-63
PCGS or NGC	MS-66

1891-CC (generic)

Collector Insights

After the peak production of silver dollars in 1890, mintages tapered off slightly in 1891 to a little more than a million and a half. But that's still near the top end of silver-dollar production at this Western branch mint. Talk about the calm before an impending storm—the Mint maintained almost the same level of production in 1892, but coinage totals dropped precipitously in 1893 to only 677,000 pieces. Of course, original mintages are not necessarily the key to how many coins exist today. In fact, more than half of all silver dollars ever struck have been melted by the U.S. government, and in the case of Carson City dollars, the question is, how many survived in government vaults? As for the 1891-CC, surprisingly few were found in the GSA hoard. It's been reported that slightly over 5,500 were put in GSA holders, which, when compared to the combined total of more than 2 million for 1882, 1883, and 1884, is a minuscule number. So, where does that leave us in terms of the 1891-CC? Simply put, this Carson City date is an important rarity when found in a GSA case, and the price it brings in the marketplace reflects intense collector demand.

Variety Notes

Mention "1891-CC" to a variety collector and you can expect to hear about the infamous Spitting Eagle variety. It made its way into the original TOP 100 book and has been there ever since. Apparently, there's no way to get this eagle out of the nest. The reason for all the discussion is that the 1891-CC VAM 3 is one of the most overrated varieties in the Morgan dollar series. More than half of all 1891-CC specimens, either in or out of a GSA holder, are of this particular variety. In addition to the VAM 3, there are a few other cataloged varieties for this date, including some mint-mark varieties, but none has generated any excitement. Maybe that's why the Spitting Eagle variety developed such a strong following. In any case, every collector needs a VAM 3 specimen to complete his or her TOP 100 set, but the fact to underscore here is this variety's ready availability. A piece of advice: never pay a premium for a Spitting Eagle.

1891-CC VAM 3

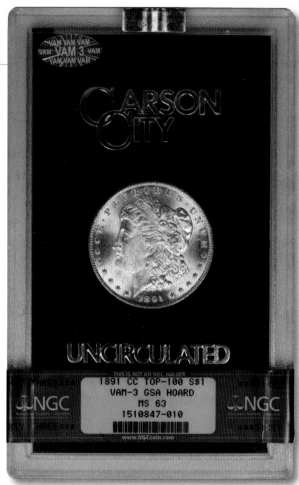

The best thing about the 1891-CC Spitting Eagle variety is its great name. However, don't be enticed, like many novice collectors, into mistakenly paying too much for this common coin.

Valuations		GSA	MS-61	MS-62	MS-63	MS-64	MS-65	MS-66	MS-67
In GSA Case	MS	$3,000	$3,250	$3,800	$5,000	$22,500			
(Graded by NGC)	PL								
	DMPL								
Slabbed	MS		450	500	900	1,500	$4,750	$15,000	$37,500
(Not in GSA Case)	PL		500	650	1,000	1,600	7,000	15,000	
	DMPL		650	1,250	2,650	7,500	30,000		

The Spitting Eagle VAM 3 is a frequently
encountered variety, but is often
promoted as a rare VAM. Don't be fooled!

Condition Census

In GSA Case	MS-64
PCGS or NGC	MS-65

Note: The professional grading services to date do not designate VAM 3. The census here is that of the authors' determination.

1891-CC VAM 3

Collector Insights

What's in a name? Everything, apparently, when it comes to numismatics. Somewhere in the mists of the distant past, someone came up with a moniker for this variety that made it a superstar. The common VAM 3 was transformed into the Spitting Eagle variety. But is it worth all the hoopla? Absolutely not. Turns out that 60 or 70 percent of *all* 1891-CC specimens entering the marketplace are found to be this particular variety. In other words, any of the other 1891-CC varieties might be considered scarce compared to the Spitting Eagle. And it is just as common in a GSA hard case. So the skinny on this coin is to avoid paying a premium for the VAM 3, either inside or out of a GSA holder. In short, the primary attraction this variety has going for it may be its name.

Variety Notes

The moniker is a good one, as Spitting Eagle certainly describes the small, teardrop-shaped die gouge that's visible in front of the eagle's beak. No one has expressed any problems in identifying this variety, and of course, a collector would typically encounter lots of examples with which to hone down his attribution skills. But to be technically complete, we should mention that the tops of the letters in the CC mintmark show clear doubling, particularly along the top of the left C. Again, we must stress the Spitting Eagle variety is worth little or no premium either inside or outside a GSA case. So don't be confused by major marketing efforts that tout the VAM 3 as an important TOP 100 variety. It was only included to focus on its availability and to save novice collectors money.

1892-CC
(GENERIC)

The 1892-CC is one of three Carson City dates
for which only one specimen was reported in
the GSA hoard. The current whereabouts
of this unique 1892-CC remain unknown.

Valuations

		GSA	MS-61	MS-62	MS-63	MS-64	MS-65	MS-66
In GSA Case	MS							
(Graded by NGC)	PL							
	DMPL							
Slabbed	MS		$1,600	$1,800	$2,500	$3,500	$9,500	$35,000
(Not in GSA Case)	PL		1,650	1,900	2,900	4,000	13,000	
	DMPL		1,800	2,800	5,500	10,000	50,000	

The actual variety is unimportant when it comes to locating the
one 1892-CC specimen reported to be part of the GSA hoard.

By the Numbers

Original Mintage	1,352,000
Total GSA Holdings	1
Percentage of Mintage in GSA	
Original Uncirculated Designation	0
Not Designated Due to Scratches/Toning etc.	1
GSA Overall Rarity Ranking	Tied 1st
Non-GSA Rarity Ranking	3rd
GSA Prooflike or DMPL Availability	Unique

Condition Census

In GSA Case	Unique Choice Uncirculated
PCGS or NGC	MS-66

1892-CC (generic)

Collector Insights

The 1892-CC is one of three Morgan dollar dates for which there is only one GSA specimen recorded. The other two are the 1889-CC and the 1893-CC. And while a single lone 1889-CC in a GSA case has been found, there hasn't been even a trace of the 1892-CC or the 1893-CC. Why? The sad truth is that the 1892-CC and 1893-CC were so valuable in their own right that along the way they likely were broken out of their GSA holders and submitted to one of the grading services for slabbing. What a tragedy! It's interesting that in the GSA sales all three unique specimens were sold in the "Mixed CC" category, because it was decided that there weren't enough of each to warrant separate listings in the main "Uncirculated CC" category. The startling irony is that the "Mixed CC" category was also the repository for scratched and tarnished pieces, so imagine the surprise of the lucky buyers who expected damaged coins, but received these one-of-a-kind rarities. Indeed, the most valuable three coins in the entire government hoard were mixed in with the more than half a million Morgan dollar "rejects"!

Variety Notes

If you were to find the one 1892-CC specimen reported as part of the GSA hoard, you probably won't care about the variety. In the first place, there are no particularly significant varieties for 1892-CC, and none is listed in either the TOP 100 or HOT 50 listings of the most important Morgan dollar varieties. But even if there *were* rare varieties dated 1892-CC, it matters little which die pair is represented since there is only one known coin in a GSA case! That said, it's conceivable that one or more 1892-CC specimens found their way anonymously into GSA soft packs as part of the government hoard. But whether you're looking for the one reported 1892-CC in a hard case or an unreported specimen in a Blue Pack, the thrill is in the searching. Who knows, like the lost Dutchman mine, it may still be possible to locate the "lost" 1892-CC GSA dollar! Hope springs eternal.

1893-CC
(GENERIC)

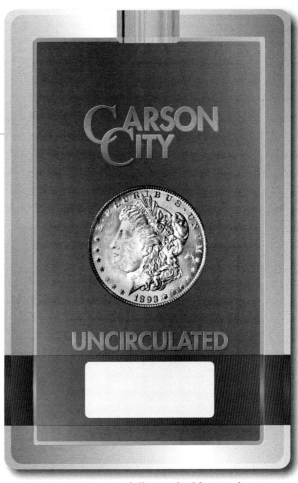

Any 1893-CC Morgan dollar is a highly prized rarity—but the number reported in the GSA hoard is exactly one! What a fitting way to close the chapter on silver-dollar production at the Carson City branch mint.

Valuations		GSA	MS-61	MS-62	MS-63	MS-64	MS-65	MS-66
In GSA Case	MS							
(Graded by NGC)	PL							
	DMPL							
Slabbed	MS		$5,000	$6,000	$8,500	$16,500	$65,000	$160,000
(Not in GSA Case)	PL		5,250	6,500	9,500	32,500	80,000	
	DMPL		6,000	10,000	20,000	45,000	85,000	

1893 was the last year the legendary CC mintmark appeared on silver dollars, ending an on-again, off-again run of 28 eventful years.

By the Numbers

Original Mintage	677,000
Total GSA Holdings	1
Percentage of Mintage in GSA	
Original Uncirculated Designation	0
Not Designated Due to Scratches/Toning etc.	1
GSA Overall Rarity Ranking	Tied 1st
Non-GSA Rarity Ranking	2nd
GSA Prooflike or DMPL Availability	Unique

Condition Census

In GSA Case	Unique Choice Uncirculated
PCGS or NGC	MS-65

1893-CC (generic)

Collector Insights

The closing of the Carson City Mint in 1893 marked the end of an era. No longer would silver from the Comstock Lode bonanza be locally struck into the cartwheels that were such an integral part of the lore and mystique of the Wild West. Even so, official records indicate that 677,000 silver dollars were struck that final year at Carson City. Some were saved as mementos, and some undoubtedly entered circulation, but most simply disappeared over time, probably as part of one massive coin melt or another. But the biggest surprise is that only one 1893-CC specimen was reported in the GSA hoard. Even today, specialists have not been able to confirm the existence of that one 1893-CC GSA dollar in any current collection. Where should we look? No one knows, since it's possible that this unique specimen could be residing in either a GSA hard plastic case or a Blue Pack envelope. Or, more likely, along the way its perceived value became so great that it was removed from its original GSA holder. If you need an incentive to find it, the untested value of the one 1893-CC in a GSA holder might be five or six figures, which should be more than enough to motivate anyone.

Variety Notes

In mid-1893, at a time when the price of silver bullion was experiencing a precipitous drop and production was declining in the nearby mines, coining operations at the Carson City Mint came to an abrupt halt by order of officials in Washington. Politics aside, the good news for today's collectors is that almost 700,000 silver dollars had already been struck, and a quick accounting indicates that at least four obverses and four reverses were used. None of the resulting die varieties, which include doubled dates and several minor doubled dies, have caught on with collectors up this point. However, the fact remains that only one 1893-CC was reported to exist in the original GSA holdings, so the actual variety becomes less than critical. Indeed, the collector who uncovers the unique GSA-encased '93-CC, whatever the variety, will undoubtedly write his own ticket to financial reward!

1900-O/CC VARIETIES

One of the most widely sought-after 1900-O/CC varieties is the VAM 9, featured here, which was the only O/CC variety to be featured separately in the Top 100 listings.

Variety Notes

The pressing need for a mint in Carson City had all but vanished by 1893, when the decreasing output of the Comstock silver mines and America's worsening economic woes worked in concert to bring the branch mint to its knees. Problems and instability at the Carson City Mint itself further served to spell disaster for its operation. Finally, in 1899 the status of the Carson City Mint was officially reduced to that of an assay office, and its three coinage presses, along with all dies and other equipment still on hand, were shipped back to the Philadelphia Mint. Then, as a footnote that still excites collectors today, a number of those returned reverse dies with the famous "CC" mintmark were repunched with an "O" mintmark and shipped the following year to the still-operating branch mint in New Orleans. The resulting 1900 "O/CC" varieties are now among the most avidly collected VAMs in the Morgan dollar series.

The Ten Known 1900-O/CC Varieties

VAM	Rarity	Variety Notes
7	Ultra-rare	No known BU's and rare in all grades; same reverse die as VAM 10
7A	Ultra-rare	Die chips on top of 9 in the date; finest known grades at only AU-58
8	Common	Stubby remains of underlying CC on right side of mintmark
8A	Common	Considerable die-rust pitting around mintmark; unmistakable
8B	Scarce	Very late die state VAM 8 with clash marks on obverse and reverse
9	Rare	Remains of underlying CC are disconnected on right side of mintmark
10	Common	Strong bottom edges of CC on both sides of mintmark
10A	Scarce	Late die state of VAM 10 with evidence of clashing on both sides
11	Common	Easily seen evidence of a C to left of mintmark
12	Common	Best remains of the underlying CC of any 1900-O/CC variety

APPENDIX A
⪥COLLECTOR'S CHECKLIST⪦

Date	VAM Variety	Grade	Service	Date of Purchase	Purchase Price	Notes
1878-CC						
1878-CC	VAM-11					
1878-CC	VAM-18					
1878-CC	VAM-24					
1879-CC						
1879-CC	VAM-3					
1880-CC						
1880-CC, 80/79, Rev of 78	VAM-4					
1880-CC, Rev of 79, High 7	VAM-5					
1880-CC, Rev of 79, Low 7	VAM-6					
1880-CC, Rev of 78	VAM-7					
1881-CC						
1881-CC	VAM-2					
1882-CC						
1882-CC	VAM-2					
1882-CC, Double-Struck						
1883-CC						
1883-CC	VAM-4					

Date	VAM Variety	Grade	Service	Date of Purchase	Purchase Price	Notes
1884-CC						
1884-CC	VAM-2					
1885-CC						
1885-CC	VAM-4					
1889-CC						
1890-CC						
1890-CC, Tail Bar	VAM-4					
1891-CC						
1891-CC, Spitting Eagle	VAM-3					
1892-CC						
1893-CC						

APPENDIX B

This appendix shows current (as of early 2014) certification populations of Carson City Morgan dollars from the GSA release—the number of coins that have been certified and graded by Numismatic Guaranty Corporation of America (NGC). This set of data gives the collector and investor a real-world snapshot of the relative rarities of different dates and VAM varieties.

1878-CC	MS-64	MS-65	MS-66	MS-67	MS-68
	704	100	3	0	0
	MS-64PL	MS-65PL	MS-66PL	MS-67PL	MS-68PL
	59	6	2	0	0
	MS-64DMPL	MS-65DMPL	MS-66DMPL	MS-67DMPL	
	2	0	0	0	

1878-CC, VAM-11	MS-62	MS-63	MS-64	MS-65	MS-66
	52	52	36	4	0
	MS-62PL	MS-63PL	MS-64PL	MS-65PL	MS-66PL
	0	4	1	0*	0
	MS-62DMPL	MS-63DMPL	MS-64DMPL	MS-65DMPL	
	1	0	0	0	

* Note: The authors have stickered an MS-65PL not designated by NGC.

1878-CC, VAM-18	MS-60	MS-61	MS-62	MS-63	MS-64
	0	2	0	0	0
	MS-60PL	MS-61PL	MS-62PL	MS-63PL	MS-64PL
	3	2	0	0	0
	MS-62DMPL	MS-63DMPL	MS-64DMPL	MS-65DMPL	
	0	0	0	0	

Note: None are known to exist in DMPL.

1878-CC, VAM-24	Note: Only a lone example has been certified, at MS-61.

1879-CC	MS-63	MS-64	MS-65	MS-66	MS-67
	196	72	7	0	0
	MS-63PL	MS-64PL	MS-65PL	MS-66PL	MS-67PL
	16	2	0	0	0
	MS-63DMPL	MS-64DMPL	MS-65DMPL	MS-66DMPL	
	0	0	0	0	

Note: None are known to exist in DMPL.

1879-CC, VAM-3	MS-63	MS-64	MS-65	MS-66	MS-67
	49	18	2	0	0
	MS-63PL	MS-64PL	MS-65PL	MS-66PL	MS-67PL
	0	0	0	0	0
	MS-63DMPL	MS-64DMPL	MS-65DMPL	MS-66DMPL	
	0	0	0	0	

Note: None are known to exist in PL or DMPL.

1880-CC*	MS-64	MS-65	MS-66	MS-67	MS-68
	2,075	708	104	1	0
	MS-64PL	MS-65PL	MS-66PL	MS-67PL	MS-68PL
	61	22	6	0	0
	MS-64DMPL	MS-65DMPL	MS-66DMPL	MS-67DMPL	
	191	30	1	0	

* Note: These 1880-CC populations include the very rare varieties of VAM-5 and VAM-6, of which VAM-6 is the rarest.

1880-CC, VAM-4 and VAM-7*	MS-64	MS-65	MS-66	MS-67	MS-68
	539	131	14	0	0
	MS-63PL	MS-64PL	MS-65PL	MS-66PL	MS-67PL
	13	9	10	0	0
	MS-63DMPL	MS-64DMPL	MS-65DMPL	MS-66DMPL	
	8	5	0	0	

* Note: These are combined populations for the rare 1880-CC VAM-4 and VAM-7 varieties, of which VAM-7 is the rarest.

1881-CC*	MS-64	MS-65	MS-66	MS-67	MS-68
	3,019	1,484	365	23	0
	MS-64PL	MS-65PL	MS-66PL	MS-67PL	MS-68PL
	121	38	3	0	0
	MS-64DMPL	MS-65DMPL	MS-66DMPL	MS-67DMPL	
	58	24	4	1	

* See below for a note about 1881-CC, VAM-2.

1881-CC, VAM-2	Note: Although NGC designates 1881-CC, VAM-2, many exist that aren't designated. Based on the authors' experience, this split is approximately 65% designated, 35% not designated.MS68DMPL				

1882-CC*

MS-64	MS-65	MS-66	MS-67	MS-68
6,077	2,310	375	10	0
MS-64PL	MS-65PL	MS-66PL	MS-67PL	MS-68PL
332	102	21	0	0
MS-64DMPL	MS-65DMPL	MS-66DMPL	MS-67DMPL	
131	32	3	0	

* See below for a note about 1882-CC, VAM-2.

1882-CC, VAM-2	Note: NGC does not designate 1882-CC, VAM-2. See the data for the generic 1882-CC, above. Based on the authors' experience, approximately 75% are generic and 25% are VAM-2.

1883-CC*

MS-64	MS-65	MS-66	MS-67	MS-68
8,730	3,935	666	26	0
MS-64PL	MS-65PL	MS-66PL	MS-67PL	MS-68PL
525	173	25	1	0
MS-64DMPL	MS-65DMPL	MS-66DMPL	MS-67DMPL	
236	76	4	2	

* See below for a note about 1883-CC, VAM-4.

1883-CC, VAM-4	Note: NGC does not designate 1883-CC, VAM-4. See the data for the generic 1883-CC, above. Based on the authors' experience, approximately 75% are generic and 25% are VAM-4.

1884-CC*

MS-64	MS-65	MS-66	MS-67	MS-68
9793	4076	653	28	0
MS-64PL	MS-65PL	MS-66PL	MS-67PL	MS-68PL
506	136	17	0	0
MS-64DMPL	MS-65DMPL	MS-66DMPL	MS-67DMPL	
231	53	8	0	

* See below for a note about 1884-CC, VAM-2.

1884-CC, VAM-2	Note: NGC does not designate 1884-CC, VAM-2. See the data for the generic 1884-CC, above. Based on the authors' experience, approximately 80% are generic and 20% are VAM-2.

1885-CC*

MS-64	MS-65	MS-66	MS-67	MS-68
2,927	1,281	281	16	0
MS-64PL	MS-65PL	MS-66PL	MS-67PL	MS-68PL
307	120	36	3	0
MS-64DMPL	MS-65DMPL	MS-66DMPL	MS-67DMPL	
32	14	1	0	

* See below for a note about 1885-CC, VAM-4.

1885-CC, VAM-4	Note: See the data for the generic 1885-CC, above. Based on the authors' experience, approximately 70% are generic and 30% are VAM-4. This variety is extremely rare in high grades.

1889-CC	Note: Unique. Certified as MS-62DMPL.

1890-CC

MS-62	MS-63	MS-64	MS-65	MS-66
260	134	13	1	0
MS-62PL	MS-63PL	MS-64PL	MS-65PL	MS-66PL
0	0	0	0	0
MS-62DMPL	MS-63DMPL	MS-64DMPL	MS-65DMPL	
0	0	0	0	

1890-CC, VAM-4	Note: Currently, none are known in a GSA holder.

1891-CC

MS-62	MS-63	MS-64	MS-65	MS-66
137	63	3	0	0
MS-62PL	MS-63PL	MS-64PL	MS-65PL	MS-66PL
0	0	0	0	0
MS-62DMPL	MS-63DMPL	MS-64DMPL	MS-65DMPL	
0	0	0	0	

1891-CC, VAM-3

MS-62	MS-63	MS-64	MS-65	MS-66
202	91	7	0	0
MS-62PL	MS-63PL	MS-64PL	MS-65PL	MS-66PL
0	0	0	0	0
MS-62DMPL	MS-63DMPL	MS-64DMPL	MS-65DMPL	
0	0	0	0	

1892-CC	Note: Although the authors have not seen an 1892-CC in a GSA case, one is believed to exist. It has probably long since been broken out of its case.

1893-CC	Note: Although the authors have not seen an 1893-CC in a GSA case, one is believed to exist. It has probably long since been broken out of its case.

ABOUT THE AUTHORS

Adam Crum was born in Dallas, Texas, and was introduced to coin collecting by his father. His fascination with the hobby's business side grew, and by the time he was 22 years old he had made it a full-time enterprise. In addition to being an avid student of U.S. numismatics, Adam has spent his career helping others understand how to successfully buy and sell U.S. coins. He has written and published a numismatic newsletter since 1991, and his articles have appeared in most of the leading numismatic publications. The coauthor of *An Insider's Guide to Collecting Type I Double Eagles*, Adam has also been a regular contributor to *A Guide Book of United States Coins* (the "Red Book") and to all editions of *100 Greatest U.S. Coins* and the *Encyclopedia of U.S. Gold Coins, 1795–1933*. His company, Monaco Rare Coins, and Numismatic Guaranty Corporation were the sole financial contributors to the building of the National Numismatic Collection's public exhibit at the Smithsonian Institution. In 2001 he successfully negotiated one of the largest transactions in U.S. numismatic history when his company purchased most of the rare gold monetary ingots and hundreds of coins recovered from the SS *Central America*.

Adam is a member of the Professional Numismatists Guild, the Numismatic Literary Guild, the American Numismatic Association (life member), and most of the leading numismatic organizations.

Selby Ungar has been active in the field of numismatics for more than 30 years. He is a certified dealer for Professional Coin Grading Service (PCGS), Numismatic Guaranty Corporation (NGC), ANACS, and Independent Coin Graders (ICG), and is a life member of the American Numismatic Association. He serves on the board of governors for the National Silver Dollar Roundtable (NSDR) and is active in many youth-oriented programs that help promote and maintain interest in numismatics. Selby has received recognition from his peers including the NSDR Man of the Year Award, and in 2003 was presented with the NSDR Lifetime Achievement Award.

Jeff Oxman is a prominent researcher, writer, speaker, editor, and specialist in silver dollars, die varieties, and VAMS, as well as a founding officer of the Society of Silver Dollar Collectors (SSDC).

Jeff's collecting interests have spanned four decades. For the past 20 years his primary focus has been Morgan and Peace dollars, and he has devoted his energies to discovering and attributing the more than 2,000 known die varieties in these series. As a result of his research, Jeff is often called upon by trade papers and organizations for his silver-dollar expertise. He is a regular contributor to the *Cherrypickers' Guide to Rare Die Varieties*.

In 1996 Jeff and coauthor Michael S. Fey released the influential *Top 100 Morgan Dollar Varieties: The VAM Keys*. A past recipient of the National Silver Dollar Roundtable (NSDR) Man of the Year Award, Jeff currently serves on the NSDR board of directors.

INDEX

Adams Brick Works, 12
Adams, Jewett W., 24
Allison, William, 17

B¹ and B² reverses, 40, 41, 45, 54
Bank of California, 5, 11
Barber, Charles, 20
Barber, William, 20
Bell, Frank, 5
Bennett, H.P., 11–12
Bland-Allison Act, 15, 17–18, 45
"Bland dollars," 22
Bland, Richard P., 17–19, 22
Bonanza Group, 6, 10
Boutwell, George S., 15
Brannan, Sam, 1–2
Bryan, William Jennings, 19
Bullion and Exchange Bank, 24
"buzzard" dollars, 22

C¹, C², and C³ reverses, 54
California Gold Rush, 1–4
Carson City, 16
Carson City Mint, 11–15, 87, 99, 105, 123
closing of, 23–25, 123, 124
construction of, 12–13, 14, 15, 17
converted to assay office, 24, 124
cost of producing coins at, 87, 91, 93
first coins struck at, 14, 45
negative publicity surrounding, 15, 23–24
rates of production at, 91, 93
Carson, Kit, 11
Carter, Amon, 27–28
"cartwheel" dollars, 15
CC mintmark, 14, 15, 53
Carson City Morgan dollars, 24–27, 33, 34, 123
in GSA cases, 35–36
hoards of (see hoards)
key date-mintmark combinations, 26
most common, 28–29, 35, 37, 96
peak production of, 114
rarity rankings, 37
ways to collect, 35–37
See also GSA mail-bid sales
Chase, Salmon P., 11
Chinese labor, 6, 8, 13
Civil War, 5, 12, 13

Coin Press No. 1, 25
Comstock area, 6
Comstock, H.T.P. "Old Pancake," 4
Comstock Lode, 4–11
Coronel, Antonio, 4
Crawford, James, 99
Curry, Abraham, 11–12, 13, 16, 17

"daddy" dollars, 22
Deidesheimer, Philip, 7
designer's initials, on U.S. coinage, 22
die states, 81, 84
die varieties, 81
dollars, paper, 25
Donner party, 2–3
Downie, "Major" William, 4
Downieville, 4

Eakins, Thomas, 21

Fair, James, 6
flat-breasted eagle, 62, 72. See also Reverse of '78,
Forty-Niners, 4
free coinage, 15
Freeman, Jim, 4

General Services Administration (GSA), 25–33. See also GSA mail-bid sales
Gobrecht, Christian, 14
gold fever, 2–4
Gold Hill, Nevada, 3
gold rushes, 4. See also California Gold Rush
gold standard, 15, 16
Gould and Curry Mine, 17
"Granite Lady," the, 12
Great Basin Hotel, 16
Green, B.F., 11
GSA mail-bid sales, 26–33, 96
Guide Book of United States Coins, A, 26–27

Haines, J.W., 9
Hal, Henry Grunt, 27–28
Harris, Hirsch, 24
Heney, James, 23
hoards
Continental Bank, 32
Redfield, 32
Treasury, 1, 87, 28

International Hotel, 8

Job, Moses and Margaret, 12
Jones, John T., 23

Klein, Jacob, 24

Liberty Seated dollar, 15
Lincoln, Abraham, 5
Linderman, Henry P., 20
Longacre, James B., 14
Lopez, Francisco, 1

Mackay, John, 6, 10
Mahler, Cliff, 27–28
Mallis, George, 32, 36
Mankin, John, 11
Marshall, James, 1, 2
McLaughlin, Pat, 4
mine owners, 15, 16. See also silver-mine lobby
miners, 6, 9
Mint Act of February 12, 1873, 15
Morgan silver dollars, 15–25, 26, 99, 108
"King of," 26–27
See also Barber, William; Morgan, George T.; Williams, Anna Willess
Morgan, George T., 20
Mormons, 6–7, 11
Mullett, Alfred B., 12–13, 14
Musser, J.J., 11

Nevada Mint Bill of 1863, 11
Nevada State Museum, 24–25
Nevada State Prison, 12
Nevada territorial prison, 17
Nevada Territory, 5, 16. See also Virginia City
Nob Hill, San Francisco, 11
Nye, James W., 12, 17

Ophir mining operation, 9, 10
O'Reilly, Peter, 4

Panic of 1873, 17
Panic of 1893, 22–23
Paquet, Anthony, 20
Peace dollars, 25
Penrod, Emmanuel, 4
Piper, Henry, 23
Pittman Act of 1918, 25
Pittman, John J., 27–28
"placer" gold, 4
Pollock, James, 11
Preston, Robert, 23
Proctor, Frank M., 11

Redfield, LaVere, 32
Reverses of '78, 63
Reverse of '79, 63, 65
Rice, H.F., 17
Riddle, James L., 12
rocker, gold, 4
Roop, Governor Isaac, 7
round-breasted eagle, 62, 72. See also Reverse of '79
Russell, Margo, 27–28

set premium, 33
Sherman, John, 15, 18, 20
Sherman Silver Purchase Act of 1890, 22
silver bullion values, 32, 108, 123
Silver Certificates, 26
Silver City, Nevada, 3
silverites, 19
silver-mine lobby, 16–17
Specie Redemption Act of 1875, 11
Spitting Eagle variety, 114–117
square-set timber supports, 7, 8
Stewart, William, 12
Sutro, Adolph, 6
Sutro Tunnel, 9–10
Sutter, Captain John A., 1, 2
Sutter's Creek, 1

Tailbar variety, 108–111
telegraph, longest in history, 5
trade dollars, 14, 15, 16
Twain, Mark, 10

Utah Territory, 6

"VAM book," the, 32, 38
VAM keys, the, 38
Van Allen, Leroy, 28, 32, 36
Van Allen-Mallis numbers, 36
V-flume, 9
Virginia and Truckee Railroad, 5, 8, 9, 17
Virginia City, 5, 8

War Time Silver Act of 1942, 25
Warm Springs Hotel, 16, 17
Williams, Anna Willess, 21

Young, Brigham, 11